All the Better to READ You With

Stories & Lessons to Inspire Reading for Pleasure

Chip Colquhoun & **Rebekah Owen**

Illustrated by **Korky Paul** & **Mario Coelho**

Foreword by **Ros Wilson**

EPIC TALES

an **immersive** experience

Dedications

For Bethany, Jan, and Luke
– *Chip*

For my Robins – past, present, and future
– *Rebekah*

Για την Κατερίνα
– *Κ.Π.*

For my late father, Luiz Gonzaga Machado Coelho,
a true community artist from Florianopolis, Brazil
– *Mario*

Foreword:
The Wonder of Storytelling

by **Ros Wilson**

If you purely seek to boost your skills as a storyteller, then this is the book for you. If, however, you would welcome a complete programme that will enhance your teaching, enrich your learners' lives with a passion for reading, and *also* boost your skills as a storyteller, then this is *definitely* the book for you!

Back in the day – about 2004 – when Big Writing was spreading like measles around the UK and the wider world, my work came in for some criticism from the world of academia. I have never forgotten the words of one children's author, who said that children should not be taught ambitious vocabulary in isolation. He thought they should learn new words the way he did: from reading widely.

Those words hurt because I'd devoted much of my 35-year career to that date teaching children new to English, children with learning difficulties, and children from severely impoverished backgrounds, and I knew that few of these children had the opportunity to immerse themselves in good quality children's literature. Many of those new to English may have read fluently in their first language, but not in English. Many of those with learning difficulties could read only the simplest of texts. And many of the impoverished had little access to books outside school.

I knew, therefore, that time was pressing – that, if there was no intervention, then the doors to success (in examinations and interviews-to-come) might never open. I also knew that many modern children's books, whilst often fun and funky, were written in quite simplistic language that would not enrich a child's language.

Now, this formidable book may have resolved those issues and concerns.

Research has proven that children who already possess a rich personal lexicon are able to understand new texts much more quickly and effectively than those who struggle to decode the many words unknown to them in almost every line. We now know, too, that word-rich children will learn more new vocabulary than word-poor children reading the same text. Adequate reading comprehension depends on the learner already knowing 90% or more of the words in the text. E D Hirsch Jr likens this to the way in which a young child acquires their early (oral) vocabulary:

"Knowing [this] percentage of words allows the reader to get the main thrust of what is being said, and therefore to guess correctly what the unfamiliar words probably mean. This inferential process is of course how we pick up oral language in early childhood, and it sustains our vocabulary growth throughout our lives."[1]

---

1 Hirsch Jr, *Reading Comprehension Requires Knowledge – of Words and the World*, 2008

On top of this, if the quality of discussion and dialogue in the home of a young child is limited by a narrow range of vocabulary and language structures, the child will only develop a restricted language base.

These factors – which I battled to illustrate twenty years ago – are now accepted by the majority of academics (although not all) and by the government. Proactive teaching of ambitious vocabulary has now become an important and accepted strategy in the world of education.

The resolution of these difficulties may be even closer than we think when educators start teaching the love of storytelling using this book.

The culture of curling up at bedtime with an adult and a delightful book is at risk of being eradicated from the lives of children today. As the generations change, the art of storytelling is in danger of becoming a thing of the past. Without role models, young children are at risk of not developing that art for themselves. They're not reading, enacting, or narrating stories to younger siblings, teddies, or Barbie. They're missing out on the joys of becoming a great storyteller. Sadly, the prescriptive early curriculum of many countries has also imposed learning to read through analytical phonics, which can sometimes kill the joy of storytelling long celebrated in the Early Years.

The magic of the first steps into reading is being crushed for many by rote learning and the fear of 'getting it wrong', which may in turn be inhibiting the *love* of reading.

So imagine my joy and delight when I first received a copy of this book and discovered that, at last, someone had married the joy of language with the delight of reading! The team's commitment to enriching children's language and vocabulary is so in tune with our *Talk:Write* programme (and my latest book, *Top Tips for Teaching Suave Words*) that I was immediately on board.

This impressive compendium combines an anthology of custom-written stories with associated lesson planning and supportive advice, all to help educators invigorate young people with a love of reading.

Being involved in the storytelling modelled and enjoyed in this book will expose children to a wealth of words which – if educators use the myriad of ideas in these teaching materials to encourage and enable their continued use in discussion – will expand their learners' vocabulary with understanding and enjoyment. Their learners will be better able to both say and use a plethora of sophisticated vocabulary.

I was lucky as a child. Not in my home background, nor in my school experiences, but rather in that, being impoverished, I only possessed three books and a few third-hand toys. But what books! The first was the Rupert the Bear Annual for 1948, which could be read at many levels. You could begin with the fun of telling the story from the pictures alone. Then, as you learned simple decoding, you could fit the dialogue from the speech bubbles into your happy narrative. Eventually, beneath each of the detailed illustrations, the story was told in small print for the emergent young reader.

My second and third books were passed to me by my eldest sister: *The Wind in the Willows* by Kenneth Graham and *The Jungle Book* by Rudyard Kipling. Both were 'real' books that engrossed me for hours, losing me in other worlds of wonder and imagination. Both were written for young children in adult language as rich and varied as any classic. I shall always be so grateful to those two authors of yesteryear for the excitement of literature that I learned from them. (My affection for *The Wind in the Willows* was so great that I stored all my collection of stunning silver papers between its pages – but you will probably need to ask your great grandmother what I am talking about...)

Each of the nine stories in this book is a joy and a delight. I had not expected to experience such pleasure in reading them. When I read the title and those opening words of '**The Mountain Inside a Molehill**' (found on page 156), I was instantly gripped with the need to know – to read on, and to explore this literary conundrum:

"Sitting at the top of a tall blue mountain somewhere underground, Saul knew he was in the worst kind of trouble. He was exhausted, alone, and defeated. If only he had listened to his mum the other day..."

I loved the natural inclusion of verse in the narrative. I loved the humour underlying the exchanges between Saul and his mother. I loved the dialogue between author and reader. And I loved the wealth of 'wonder words' – such as bait, imprisoned, grimaced, and tenaciously – that form a natural part of the accessible but rich language of the story.

I also really valued the way the supportive teaching materials prepared the educator with the guidance and advice needed to bring each story to life for their eager learners whilst enabling full access and understanding. And throughout this treasure, the illustrations bring a warmth and humour that enrich the storytelling journey.

This book brings back that wondrous experience of being clustered together in the story corner, absorbed in the wonder of storytelling. The shared enjoyment of fantasy during the school day is returning – to restore the magic of reading, and fill children's imaginations with ideas and wonders for later discussion, exploration, retelling, and roleplay. This book is a treasure trove for an educator wishing to instil a love of language and of storytelling in young minds – minds which may otherwise suffer the deprivations of life in an overcrowded world of technology.

– Ros

Contents

Foreword: The Wonder of Storytelling iii

Introduction: "What a big book you've got!" 1

Section 1: For Proof That This Book Works, Start Here 5

    Chapter 1: The Story of *Little Red Homo Sapiens* 6
        Chapter 2: A Brush With Life 11
        Chapter 3: Every Story Needs a B, M, and E 17
        Chapter 4: Reaching the Reluctant Reader 22

Section 2: Reading Like a Storyteller 27
        Chapter 5: This is NOT a Performance 29
        Chapter 6: Doing All the VOICE 34

Section 3: Stories and Lessons 41
        How to Use This Section 41

Story Volume A: Universal 47

The Story of 'Huh' 48
Lesson A1: The Most Important Invention Ever! (I) 56
Lesson A1: Behind the Scenes 58
Lesson A2: Building a Story Cave 60
Lesson A2: Behind the Scenes 63

The Story of 'Through the Forest' 65
Lesson A3: Fun on the Page 70
Worksheet: Magpie Sheet 72
Lesson A3: Behind the Scenes 73
Lesson A4: Story Links (I) 74
Worksheet: 'Through the Forest' Reading Journal 77
Lesson A4: Behind the Scenes 78

The Story of 'One Lost Slipper' 79
Lesson A5: Where Stories Come From (I) 92
Worksheet: True v Imagined 94
Lesson A5: Behind the Scenes 95
Lesson A6: What a Story Needs 96
Worksheet: "I don't like it / but" for 'One Lost Slipper' 99
'One Lost Slipper': Alternative Endings 100
Lesson A6: Behind the Scenes 102

The Story of 'Tiger's Terror' 104
Lesson A7: Where Stories Comes From (II) 108
Lesson A7: Behind the Scenes 111
Lesson A8: Story Links (II) 112
Worksheet: Story Match! 115
Worksheet: Book Finder 116

The Story of 'The REAL King of the Jungle' 117
Lesson A9: What's Going to Happen? (I) 128
Lesson A9: Behind the Scenes 130
Lesson A10: What's Going to Happen? (II) 132
Worksheet: Class Read Finder 135
Lesson A10: Behind the Scenes 136

Story Volume B: Upper 137

The Story of 'Huh, Part 2' 138
Lesson B1: The Most Important Invention Ever! (II) 146
Lesson B1: Behind the Scenes 149
Lesson B2: We Need Stories 150
Worksheet: Survival Test! 153
Lesson B2: Behind the Scenes 154

The Story of 'The Mountain Inside a Molehill' 156
Lesson B3: Where Stories Come From (III) 170
Lesson B3: Behind the Scenes 173

The Story of 'The Shapeshifter' 174
Lesson B4: Where Stories Come From (IV) 184
Worksheet: Words that Shakespeare made up! 187
Worksheet: Puck in 'The Shapeshifter' vs Puck in *A Midsummer Night's Dream* 188

The Story of 'Seething at the Sea' 189
Lesson B5: Stories Need Us... 196
Lesson B5: Behind the Scenes 198

Final Words? What Next 200

Appendix: Recyclable Lessons 203
Recyclable Lesson 1: Fun on the Page 204
Recyclable Lesson 2: What a Story Needs 206
Worksheet: Recyclable "I don't like it / but" 209
Recyclable Lesson 3: We Need Stories 210

Acknowledgements 212

About Your Storytellers 215

Introduction:
"What a big book you've got!"

The warmest of greetings to you! If Science is to be believed, you have here one of the most important books an educator can use – because it's meticulously designed to grow your learners' enthusiasm for reading, and it uses the most effective *natural* teaching tool: *storytelling*.

That's a bold statement to begin with, we know – but if you go through the first few chapters one by one, you'll soon have proof that it's true. At the halfway point, you'll feel confident that *you* can use this incredible teaching tool. And, by the end, you'll have witnessed your learners benefitting from it.

In this introduction, we'll quickly sum up the benefits of reading for pleasure ("A Worthwhile Struggle..."), acknowledge the difficulties of *achieving* those benefits ("...but a Struggle Nonetheless"), and then explain how *this book is different* (with the relatively unimaginative subheading, "**How This Book is Different**"). We'll also suggest the best ways to use this book, based on where you feel you're starting from ("**What To Do Now**").

But we'll keep this intro brief. After all, like you, we're most desperate to see your learners getting the best from their time in education – and that means helping them to reap the mahoosive rewards of reading *for pleasure*.

A Worthwhile Struggle...

Wherever you stand, there's no doubting those benefits. Even 25 years before the UCL Institute of Education hit UK national headlines in 2013 with their study revealing that **"children's leisure reading is important for educational attainment"**[1], researchers conducting the first nationwide test of American high school students observed that "17-year-olds who knew more, read more."[2]

---

1 Sullivan & Brown, *Social inequalities in cognitive scores at age 16: The role of reading*, 2013

2 Krashen, *The Power of Reading: Insights from the Research*, 2004, referring to Ravitch & Finn, *What Do Our 17-Year-Olds Know?: A Report on the First National Assessment of History and Literature*, 1987

The IoE's study was still notable, though, for two key reasons. For one, it was the first to prove that reading *for pleasure* "had a substantial influence on cognitive progress" in three areas: vocabulary (but of course), spelling (yeah, that's pretty obvious too) and maths (wait – *what?!*).

Yep: recreational readers were shown to have higher *cross-curricular* attainment. A logical explanation for this could have been that learners from better socio-economic backgrounds were likely to receive more encouragement from their parents to read, and thus also receive greater support with (and/or investment in) their education.

But the researchers wondered that too. Hence the second reason their study was notable: they found firm evidence that, **"The influence of reading for pleasure was greater than that for having a parent with a degree"**.

Significantly, many other researchers have suggested that the benefits of reading for pleasure are amplified when reading books *designed* for pleasure. One report concluded, for instance, that "Analysing data from more than 250,000 teenagers from across 35 industrialised countries, we find evidence of a sizeable 'fiction effect'; young people who read this type of text frequently have significantly stronger reading skills than their peers who do not. In contrast, the same does not hold true for the four other text types [i.e. magazines, non-fiction, newspapers, and comics]. We therefore conclude that encouraging young people to read fiction may be particularly beneficial for their reading skills."[3]

Educational attainment isn't the only benefit of reading, either. **It's been shown to reduce blood pressure and heart rate to the same** (extremely beneficial) extent as yoga[4], and there's overwhelming evidence that those who grow old with a love of reading suffer from fewer impairments to their memory and mental health.[5]

...but a Struggle Nonetheless

So of course it wasn't long after the IoE study (at least, by political standards...) before reading for pleasure became part of the UK's National Curriculum.

---

3   Jerrim & Moss, *The link between fiction and teenagers' reading skills: International evidence from the OECD PISA study*, 2018

4   Rizzolo et al, *Stress Management Strategies For Students: The Immediate Effects Of Yoga, Humor, And Reading On Stress*, 2009

5   Oh so many! Chang et al, *Reading activity prevents long-term decline in cognitive function in older people: evidence from a 14-year longitudinal study*, 2021; Stine-Morrow et al, *The Effects of Sustained Literacy Engagement on Cognition and Sentence Processing Among Older Adults*, 2022; Sun et al, *Early Childhood Reading for Pleasure: Evidence from the ABCD Study for Benefits to Cognitive Performance and Mental Health and Associated Changes in Brain Structure*, 2022... Y'know, maybe we should've given up on footnotes, and opted for a bibliography instead...

However, while reading attainment has since increased by 9% (2016–2022), the most recent assessments available as we write this book suggest that 25% of the UK's 11-year-olds are still failing to hit expected standards in reading – and that a whopping *41%* are falling short of the combined standards of reading, writing, and maths.[6]

If the UK's national level of achievement continues to improve at the same rate (1.5% per year), it will be too slow for far too many generations of learners.

Moreover, a recent research paper commissioned by the National Literacy Trust reported that young people's pleasure in reading had actually *dropped* by almost 11% over the same period![7] In 2022, that put the proportion of young recreational readers at less than half (47.8%).

So what's going on? We're giving learners time to read recreationally, we're letting them choose what they read, and we're modelling the practice – but while reading standards are edging up, reading *enjoyment* seems to be nosediving. And all the while, all those incredible benefits from reading that are regularly confirmed by researchers still appear frustratingly far off.

An answer may be gleaned from a recent Australian study, in which 896 learners between the ages of 4 and 17 were given a period of 15 minutes each day to read their own choice of "books that they might gain pleasure from reading".[8] Their teachers were expected to model the practice at the same time, and parents were encouraged to do the same at home.

When the researchers surveyed the educators at the end, 85% said they had noticed improvements in their learners' skill development and wellbeing – but *41%* reported difficulties in getting their learners to engage with the task. Avoidance techniques exhibited by the learners included chatting, time-wasting, and merely pretending to read.

So the learners weren't being *taught* to read for pleasure. They were simply being given the *opportunity*. From the learners' point-of-view, this probably felt less like encouragement to read for pleasure, and more like encouragement to *read*. In other words, if they didn't have the motivation at the outset, this period of autonomy was simply taken as a chance to chat, shift about, daydream, etc.

But... how can we *teach* reading for pleasure?

This book is here with a way that works.

How This Book is Different

We reckon you'll find several ways in which this book stands out. For starters, while the subtitle lets you know this is a book for educators, Korky Paul's colourful and playful cover means your learners won't be put off by you reading it aloud in front of them as if it's an ordinary anthology of children's stories.

And it *is* an anthology of children's stories – just not an ordinary one. You have here a collection of nine gorgeously illustrated fables and fairy tales written specifically for the purpose of being read out loud, the majority of which have been proven to engage all ages from 5 to 12.

What makes this book *extra*ordinary is that the stories are accompanied by a detailed scheme of lessons, designed and tested to unite the concepts of *reading* and *pleasure* in the minds of your learners.

---

6   UK Dept. for Education, *Academic year 2021/22: Key stage 2 attainment*, 2022

7   Cole et al, *Children and young people's reading engagement in 2022: Continuing insight into the impact of the Covid-19 pandemic on reading*, 2022

8   Collins et al, *Teachers' perceptions of the benefits and challenges of a whole-school reading for pleasure program*, 2022

If you're wondering how materials suitable for a learner as young as 5 could still be suitable for a learner aged 12, and vice versa, remember:

Reading for pleasure isn't a gradable skill, it's a *mindset*. That simple fact means that it can be cultivated at *any* age.

You may wish to make minor adjustments to each lesson based on your experience with your learners (and **Section 2** provides some advice on this), but we've found that the materials in this book provide the most rock-solid foundation. And since the pleasure of reading is attainable at any age, so too is the pleasure of this lesson scheme.

And if you're worried about your ability to engage your learners with your reading, then fear not: we've dedicated an entire section of this book to equipping you with the most enthralling techniques used by professional storytellers. And by that we mean folks who've lived and breathed storytelling *virtually their entire professional life*. Not academics; not actors; not even authors who later added oral presentation to their skillset (as you'll read later, storytelling is most definitely *not* about giving a performance). Storytellers first and foremost.

In this book, you won't find dry, dispassionate tips based purely on academic research, where attainment is the sole aim. Instead, you'll discover captivating practices based on lifetimes of experience, where enjoyment is the *main* aim – and where high academic attainment is simply a universal (and welcome!) side-effect.

What To Do Now

If you can't wait for your learners to harvest the huge heap of benefits to their education, health, and wellbeing that arises from reading for pleasure, this book has been designed to let you turn to a story and instantly engage your learners in a wondrous tale. You could do that *right now* if you feel able – and on the pages immediately after each tale, you'll then have one or two ready-to-go lesson plans to stoke an enthusiasm for reading among your learners. If that's you, flick straight to **Section 3: Stories & Lessons**!

If you'd appreciate a little guidance on how to read these tales aloud in a way that has enraptured even the most reluctant of listeners – *or if you perhaps feel **too** confident in your ability to engage learners with your reading* – then make sure you stop by **Section 2: Reading Like a Storyteller**.

But if you have any doubts at all of this book succeeding with your learners, we highly recommend that you start with **Section 1**, which we've descriptively subtitled **For Proof This Book Works, Start Here**. As we mentioned at the outset of this Introduction, storytelling is the most effective *and natural* teaching tool – but rather than presenting you with a further feast of footnotes, Section 1 will provide you with palpable proof. Just be sure to read *every* chapter in that section, *especially* Chapter 1. Start there, and we guarantee you'll end this book with *everything* you need to encourage your learners to read for pleasure: the resources, the techniques, *and* the understanding.

Whichever way you choose to use this book, though, we hope *you* enjoy it yourself as well! While it is common wisdom that learners learn best when they're having fun, it's just as true that educators educate best when *they're* having fun.

So with that in mind, let us share a story...

Section 1:

For Proof That This Book Works, Start Here

Before we share any of the theory, techniques, or resources for encouraging your learners to read for pleasure, please sit back, relax, and enjoy the story in Chapter 1.

For those who are desperate to dig out the benefits at the heart of this book, don't worry. There *is* a point to us beginning with a story, and with this story in particular – and if you skip it, you risk reducing the impact on your learners when you implement the techniques and resources later in this book.

However, right now, all you need to do is get comfy and enjoy a story written especially for you. This one isn't written to read aloud to your learners – it's for you to enjoy in your own head. If you want to encourage your learners to read for pleasure, it's vital to try reading for pleasure *yourself* – and over the page, we invite you to do just that...

Chapter 1:
The Little Red Homo Sapiens

Based on an American folk tale first collected by Mary Mapes Dodge in 1874
Adapted & written by Chip Colquhoun
Illustrated by Korky Paul

Somewhere between 40,000 and 50,000 years ago, the world began to get very cold indeed. Ice and snow covered huge swathes of the land, and many species of animal were struggling to survive.

Among those animals were four species of cavepeople, each of which lived in a cave on the side of a mountain, and each of which had a nominated leader. One species, the Homo Sapiens, looked a lot like you and me – except a bit hairier, and unashamedly wearing fur. In a language long since forgotten, their leader's name was Huh, which meant, "Oo, that's interesting!"

In the next cave along from the Homo Sapiens lived the Neanderthals. This species *also* looked a lot like you and me, except a *lot* hairier, rather more muscular, and also unabashedly wearing fur. In that language long since forgotten, their leader's name was Nuh, which meant, "*Nuffink gits in my way!*"

In the next cave along from the Neanderthals lived the Denisovans. This species *probably* looked a lot like you and me, but it was difficult to tell – because they *really* loved wearing fur. They wrapped themselves up from head to toe in the finest, fluffiest furry onesies. Their leader's name was Dennis, which meant, "Look at my lovely fur!"

In the final cave lived the Floresiensies. This species *sort of* looked like you and me, except *way* hairier, quite a bit shorter, and with ma*hoo*sive feet. Their leader's name was Florence, which meant, "Don't I have *big feet!*"

For several thousands of years, successive generations of each of these species had made tools to hunt, used fire to cook food, and chilled out in their caves. But now, temperatures had plummeted so far that each species was struggling to find prey, used fire to keep as warm as they could, and *shivered* in their caves.

One day, though, Huh was looking out from the mouth of his cave when he noticed that birds were happily eating the seeds from the tall grasses. In a language long since forgotten, he said, "Oo, that's interesting!"

Eventually, Huh's curiosity took him out of his cave. He gathered a handful of those seeds for himself, popped them into his mouth, and chewed.

Seconds later, he screwed up his face, and spat the mushed mess down by the fire. In that language long since forgotten, he said, "*Eyeuhk!*"

A little while later, Huh looked down at that mushy mess – and saw it had puffed up. "Oo!" he said. "That's interesting!"

He picked up the puffed-up mush, and gave it a sniff. Then he gave it a lick. Then he bit off a chunk and chewed.

"Oo!" he said. "That's... tasty!"

Huh sat and thought. The puffy mush was tasty food. It had come from the grass seeds, which definitely *weren't* tasty food. But there were *many* grass seeds. That could make *very* many tasty puffy mushes.

Maybe even enough to save his species, and every other species on the mountain!

Excitedly, Huh jumped up, and wrapped himself in his favourite red fur. Then he clambered along the mountainside until he was within earshot of all the species of cavepeople.

In that language long since forgotten, Huh cried, "Who will help me gather grass seed? I have seen it turn into tasty food, and I think we can make it do it again!"

"Not me!" Nuh said, then added, "Gather grass seeds? Silly Homo Sapiens. Soon I go hunt! *Nuffink gits in my way!*"

"Not me!" Dennis said, then added, "Look at my lovely fur!"

"Not me!" Florence said, then added, "Don't I have *big feet!*"

But Huh's own species listened to Huh's experience, and considered Huh's hypothesis. So Huh and the Homo Sapiens gathered plenty of grass seeds, all by themselves.

Next, Huh remembered that the seeds needed making into a mush. But chewing up all those seeds would be long, hard work – and disgusting. He figured it would go quicker if he could use something bigger than his mouth to crush them…

…like a bone from a rhino leg! Rhino leg bones were super strong – that's why the Homo Sapiens used them as clubs. He was pretty sure the other species of cavepeople had them too – so he wrapped himself in his favourite red fur, and clambered along the mountainside until he was within everyone's earshot.

In that language long since forgotten, Huh cried, "Who will help me mash the grass seeds? I have seen it turn into tasty food, and I think we can make it do it again!"

"Not me!" Nuh said, then added, "Mash grass seeds? Silly Homo Sapiens. I use *my* rhino bone to go hunt! *Nuffink gits in my way!*"

"Not me!" Dennis said, then added, "Look at my lovely fur!"

"Not me!" Florence said, then added, "Don't I have *big feet!*"

But Huh's own species listened to Huh's experience, and considered Huh's hypothesis. So Huh and the Homo Sapiens mashed up the grass seeds using rhino leg bones, all by themselves.

Next, Huh remembered the mashed seeds needed to be by the fire – so he scooped up some of the mash and placed it by the fire.

Nothing happened.

A day later, still nothing had happened.

Two days later, *still* nothing had happened.

Huh frowned. The seeds had definitely changed into the tasty puffy stuff after he'd chewed them up and left them next to the f–

"Oo!" Huh exclaimed as a realisation hit him: his mouth was wet! Had some of the wetness from his mouth got mixed in with the seedy mush? "Oo oo oo!" he added. "*That's* interesting…!"

Almost bursting with elation, Huh again wrapped himself in his favourite red fur and clambered along the mountainside.

Once within earshot of all the species of cavepeople, Huh cried, "Who will help me fetch water to bake the grass seed mush? I have seen it turn into tasty food, and I think we can make it do it again!"

"Not me!" Nuh said, then added, "Water and bake grass seeds? Silly Homo Sapiens. Soon I go hunt! I'm bound to find food soon. *Nuffink gits in my way!*"

"Not me!" Dennis said, then added, "Look at my lovely fur!"

"Not me!" Florence said, then added, "Don't I have *big feet!*"

But Huh's own species listened to Huh's experience, and considered Huh's hypothesis. So Huh and the Homo Sapiens used some spare mammoth skulls to fetch water from the nearby river before sprinkling it all over the seedy mush, all by themselves.

Sure enough, just a few hours later, the damp seedy mush beside the fire puffed up into a golden, crusty parcel. When the other members of Huh's species tried it, they all agreed that this was the best invention since… well, ever! In fact, everyone reckoned no invention would ever be better.

And so they listened to Huh's instructions for how to make it, and set to work making more.

Over time, Huh and his Homo Sapiens successors produced many millions more crusty, puffy mushes by learning to farm that grass seed – and produced many millions more generations of Homo Sapiens too.

But Nuh, Dennis, and Florence never got around to it – and so, one by one, each of *their* species went extinct…

Chapter 2:
A Brush With Life

Right now, you may be forgiven for wondering what on Earth the origin of baking has to do with reading, let alone reading for pleasure. Don't worry, all will be revealed – soon...

But first, grab something to write with. You're now going to take a test.

Do not skip this! **We cannot stress enough the importance of you completing this next activity if you want your learners to become fervently recreational readers – and you must do so before proceeding any further through this book.** If you can't grab a pen and/or paper, use a smart device or computer. If you don't have *any* of these things to hand right now, return when you do.

Also note: **this is a proper test!** For you to get the most out of this activity, and your learners to get the most out of this *book*, you **must not** refer back to Chapter 1. Rely on your memory alone.

That said, if you're not sure you recall the answer to a question, *guess* – **guessing is OK, passing is forbidden.** As teachers have told many a young learner, you might score a mark if you *guess* the answer to a question – but you'll definitely score *no* mark at all if you *don't* answer a question (and yes, that includes writing "Don't know," etc).

So just to be clear, the three rules for this test are...

> **Rule 1: Don't skip this test!**
> **Rule 2: Don't cheat.**
> **Rule 3: If you're not sure, *guess*.**

When you're able and ready to write your answers, start attempting the questions...

Little Red Homo Sapiens Quiz

1.
What were the catchphrases of the three cavepeople named below?
(Max 3 marks)

Nuh

Dennis

Florence

2.
Which species had the largest cave?
(Max 1 mark)

3.
What did the Homo Sapiens use to mash the grass seeds?
(Max 1 mark)

4.
Apart from Huh, what colour furs did the other cavepeople wear?
(Max 3 marks)

5.
What extra ingredient needed adding to the seeds before the fire would puff them up?
(Max 1 mark)

6.
How did Huh feel about the fact that his species was the only one to survive?
(Max 1 mark)

How do you think you did? Remember, you mustn't have any blank spaces – if you can't recall or aren't sure, *guess*. Don't look back to the story – just quickly make something up, then read on.

Keep hold of your answers – we'll check them in a bit. But right now, let's return to our bold assertion at the start of our introduction: that this book *will* help your learners grow a love of reading through the use of storytelling. How can we be so sure of that?

Case Studies

We could offer our personal experience. Bex, the teacher trainer at work on this book, has used storytelling for many years in her classroom. She finds that removing the barrier of reading for her most reluctant readers enables them to feel the enjoyment of stories. The result? Those learners grow more excited about reading independently.

Then there are the thousands of teachers worldwide who have claimed that a storyteller's visit to their school helped their learners to swiftly and vastly improve their writing, historical knowledge, mathematical prowess, and more (and in future handbooks, we hope to share how to secure *those* benefits for your learners with storytelling too). Chip, the storyteller at work on this book, has received his fair share of that feedback – but most relevant to *this* handbook are two comments that he received from *parents*.

The first is from 2016, when Chip was asked to tell stories for an after-school 'pyjama party' for families who attended St Andrew's Primary School in Soham, Cambridgeshire. This meant two hours of leading chocolate-fuelled children through a variety of hilarious, adventurous, and inspiring stories – all told off the top of Chip's head, as is the way of traditional storytelling. He wasn't reading any stories, nor was he remembering any scripts. The tales were drawn from folklore found all around the world, so they weren't made up on the spot – but the words spoken *were* improvised, meaning that those children received a truly unique performance.

The following week, a mum by the name of Kate felt compelled to contact Chip and say, "Over the weekend, my son Luke chose to put on his reading glasses and begin reading, all by himself. He's never done that without a struggle before, so I asked why he was doing it now on his own, and he just said, 'I want more stories!' So thank you – you inspired him!"

Just like that, *telling* stories had inspired a child to start *reading* them. And remember, Chip hadn't been *reciting* a book, let alone reading one. The child had made the connection from stories to books *independently*.

The second is more recent. Chip was telling stories for an online event arranged by the Museum of Cambridge, as part of the museum's provision to its community during one of the UK's first covid lockdowns. This was similar to the pyjama party, except that Chip's ability to connect with his audience was of course far more limited. They could see and hear him, but he could not see his audience. He could only read the reactions they took time to share in a chat box down one side of the screen.

Even so, those messages revealed a high level of participation from the audience – including Jan, a young lad with English as an additional language who was celebrating his sixth birthday. Jan's parents were so awed by their son's engagement with this event that they searched for Chip online. They promptly bought one of Chip's books for children, in the hope of encouraging Jan to read more – and to do so in English.

It was only when the book arrived that they considered they may have acted a bit prematurely. The book was in fact a *history* book, contained just a couple of black and white illustrations per chapter, and was on a subject most learners in the UK don't explore until at least the age of 7. And at 220 pages, it was ten times thicker than the books their son was bringing back from school to read – with far more words per page, too.

But to their surprise, 6-year-old Jan eagerly took that book and began reading it. His mother Joanna later excitedly contacted Chip to say, "He hardly put it down until he finished. He's since taken it to show his teachers, and they were amazed. His reading has improved so much since, it's wonderful."

So storytelling has definitely, and seemingly *effortlessly*, inspired young people to read – including reluctant readers, and those for whom their book of choice isn't in their first language.

Historical Proof

Of course, such anecdotal evidence is all very well, but it's also selective and subjective by nature. A scientist would want a larger sample size – so how about every human who's ever existed since the agricultural revolution of 10,000+ years BC?

This was the inspiration for the story you read in Chapter 1. Chip took *The Little Red Hen*, an American folk tale that gained global popularity after it was first captured in print by Mary Mapes Dodge, and adapted it to weave in actual anthropological findings. Sure, this meant taking a few liberties with the historical and geographical facts – while those four species of cavepeople may have overlapped chronologically, it's incredibly unlikely they all had a cave on the side of the same mountain. But the general gist follows the evidence: Homo Sapiens (otherwise known as 'humanity') was the only species of cavepeople to work out that the seeds of grassy crops could be processed into something edible – and, importantly, *plentiful*.

Moreover, largely thanks to this discovery, humanity is the only species of cavepeople still around today.

If you try reverse-engineering a loaf of bread, you'll soon realise that the discovery of baking required a lot more brainpower than the other inventions of the Stone Age. While the Little Red Hen follows a very well-known recipe, the first human bakers required a level of consideration and communication that, until that moment in time, seems to have been unprecedented in human nature – indeed, nature as a whole. The complexity of the process would have required detailed observation, hypothesising, and *hope*.

In that, we can also see the structure of storytelling: an existing setting (the observation), a likely outcome (the hypothesis), and a problem to be solved (the hope). Altogether, these necessitated the development of humanity's irrefutably essential survival skill: *imagination*.

Tens of thousands of years on, we'll probably never know for certain which came first. Did the agricultural revolution provide the foundation for the imagination, or vice versa? (NB: The story of '**Huh, Part 2**', for your learners to enjoy in **Section 3**, presents an alternative suggestion for how the imagination developed.)

Whichever way around it happened, the result is that, stemming from this massively significant development in the survival of our species, every human being today has an entirely natural attraction to story. From the moment we start understanding language *if not before*, we're intrinsically tuned to gather and retain information gleaned through stories – and the more we do so, the more we *want* to do so.

Palpable Proof

But don't feel you have to take our word for it. Our experiences offer some evidence; the conclusions of anthropologists offer yet more. But nothing is going to be more convincing than your *own* experience.

So let's *have* that experience – right now! Pull out your answers to the *Little Red Homo Sapiens* quiz from a couple of subheadings ago – but we'll start by focusing on *your odd-numbered answers only*.

Give yourself a mark for every answer you got right. Your answers don't have to match ours word-for-word – we'll let you decide whether you deserve a mark (or a half-mark) – but be honest with yourself.

Here, then, are the answers to *the odd-numbered questions only*:

1.
Nuh: "Nuffink gits in my way!"
Dennis: "Look at my lovely fur!"
Florence: "Don't I have big feet!"

3.
Rhino bone.

5.
Water. (NB: we'll accept 'spit'.)

Max. 5 marks.

So how did you do?

Remember: if you've followed our instructions exactly, you enjoyed that story once, you were enjoying it for the first time, and you enjoyed it without expecting a test – and yet *you've remembered swathes of detail without intentionally trying to.*

This is clear evidence for the power of storytelling on a human mind: when you encounter a story, you can't help but begin to draw it into your memory.

The Brain as a Sponge?

Psychologists attest to this in their abundance. In his Pulitzer Prize Finalist book, cognitive psychologist Steven Pinker wrote, "The rush of intoxication a good story triggers doesn't make us closet hedonists – it makes us willing pupils, primed to absorb the myriad lessons each story imparts."[1] And pioneering evolutionary psychologists Leda Cosmides and John Tooby wrote an even more saucy quote: "Recent breakthroughs in neuroscience reveal that our brain is hardwired to respond to story; the pleasure we derive from a tale well told is nature's way of seducing us into paying attention to it."[2]

From this comes the popular distillation of neurology that, presented with a story, a brain becomes something like a sponge or a mop, absorbing as much new information as it can hold.

But we're not happy with that metaphor, because there's a whole lot more to it than that. Sure, as you now have evidence for, your brain will soak up the detail found within a story. But let's now take a look at your *even-numbered* answers to the quiz...

---

1   Pinker, *How the Mind Works*, 1997

2   Cosmides & Tooby, "Does Beauty Build Adapted Minds? Toward an Evolutionary Theory of Aesthetics, Fiction and the Arts", from *SubStance* Vol 30 No 1, 2001

A Better Metaphor

Again, if you followed our instructions exactly, you should have an answer to every even-numbered question – even though *the information for those questions was not provided in Chip's story*.

Who had the largest cave? That was your choice. What colours did the other cavepeople wear? You answered with what you imagined. How did Huh feel about his species being the only one to survive? That feeling was created *by you*.

Your even-numbered answers are your proof that you *do* have an imagination. You *actively contributed* to the story.

This is what makes storytelling an immensely effective tool for engagement and learning. Not only do you draw on a story for information, but you draw on it for *inspiration*, automatically adding the detail you need to feel immersed in the story. When you read or hear a tale, you're as much a creator as the storyteller, if not more so, because you are creating the characters and the world they inhabit *within your own mind*.

Because your creativity is at once linked to the story and expanding upon it, your mind is simultaneously focused on the tale while developing the ability to create independently of it. This is also the definition of 'critical thinking': using what you have in front of you to form your own ideas.

That's the beauty of how the human mind evolved: the more it reflected on past realities, the more it grew the capacity to create future possibilities.

Again, today's top scientists flock to this conclusion. Leading neuroscientist Michael Gazzaniga wrote, "Story is what enabled us to imagine what might happen in the future, and so prepare for it – a feat no other species can lay claim to, opposable thumbs or not."[3]

And so, rather than think of the brain like a sponge, we suggest it should be thought of as a *paintbrush*: just as absorbent, but where the absorption enables acts of originality.

So what could be a better teaching tool than this, a method that naturally stimulates effective memory, critical thinking, and creativity, all while being highly engaging?

Putting the Roof on the Proof

Despite everything we've mentioned here, we know there will be some educators whose experience *in the classroom* seems to contradict these principles. Perhaps they've seen learners quickly disengage from a story that didn't match their interests. Perhaps their learners seemed somewhat engaged for the first chapter or so, but then grew 'tired' of it. Or perhaps their learners have been put off by a constant struggle with language.

We'll cover the likely reasons for these engagement struggles in **Chapter 4** – and, more importantly, we'll explain how the stories in this book can help you overcome those struggles. To lay the foundations for that chapter, though, in **Chapter 3** we'll first explore exactly what any story needs in order to be truly engaging...

[3] Gazzaniga, *Human: The Science Behind What Makes Your Brain Unique*, 2009

Chapter 3:
Every Story Needs a B, M, and E...

So what is it about stories that makes them so engaging, compelling, and moreish? Why have children, after just an hour of live storytelling in person *or* online, found themselves so hungry for stories that they later avidly reached for reading glasses they had hitherto avoided, or bravely began a book ten times the size of those they were being given to read by their teacher?

To help us answer these questions, let's break down the concept of story into its essential components: B, M, and E.

Narrative Structure

Many learners young and old will have heard an erudite voice wisely tell them, "Every story needs a beginning, a middle, and an end."

So isn't it unfortunate that so many writers either didn't hear or completely ignored that advice. Take a little-known playwright from the era of Elizabeth I, for instance, by the name of William Shakespeare. Hardly any of his plays had a beginning. He insisted on dropping his audiences right in the middle of the action, the middle of an argument, sometimes the middle of a tempest. If only he'd known that stories needed beginnings – then perhaps his plays would still be popular today.

Then there was a very promising screenwriter in the 1960s by the name of Tony Warren. His series, *Coronation Street*, now holds a Guinness World Record for being the longest running TV soap opera. If only he'd known that stories needed endings – then maybe *Coronation Street* would still be popular today.

Hold on a mo'...

OK, perhaps we're being unfair to proponents of the 'Beginning, Middle, and End' principle. Shakespeare's preference to 'begin in the middle' still involves beginning somewhere. Soap operas like *Coronation Street* are tapestries of storylines, many of which ended years ago. But there's definitely more to stories than just starting, going on for a bit, and then finishing.

Take a day in the life of Lady A. She wakes up one weekend and decides to visit her friend Lady B. After the short walk between their homes, Lady A calls on Lady B, and is welcomed inside. They chat, drink tea, and then Lady A heads home.

Lady A's day has a beginning, middle, and end. Does that make it a *story* though? Probably not the kind you'd rush to buy from a bookshop, or download from your favourite streaming service.

Your learners would almost certainly feel the same. That's not to say they wouldn't find Lady A's day engaging and memorable if you told it to them using a rich profusion of rhetorical devices, such as actions, rhythm, and rhyme. But in that event, it would be more accurate to say that they are engaging with *you*, not the tale – so they'd be unlikely to come away with a thirst for story, let alone reading.

The emphasis on having a 'beginning, middle, and end' is true for crafting a *narrative structure* – but it's really rather unhelpful when it comes to identifying what makes a story compelling. If learners have only this structure to go on, they should be forgiven for struggling to engage with a story, or be inspired by it, much less come up with an interesting or entertaining idea for a story of their own.

But the letters B, M, and E *can* stand for the three essential elements of *stories* – the aspects that hook us in, *reel* us in, and then lodge that story in our memories for days if not *decades* to come. Using what we know about the role of stories in the survival of humanity, let's redefine the B, M, and E...

B for 'Bad Things Need to Happen'

Can you think of a highly popular story where nothing bad happens?

We confidently predict that you can't. Chip has travelled both hemispheres telling stories, and he's asked this question wherever he's gone. No-one has given him such a story – because no-one can.

If you think *you* can, do please write in. But every fairy tale, every legend, every bestseller, every blockbuster on a stage or silver screen... If it's a story, it's pretty much a given that *something bad happens*. Even Peppa Pig is constantly having to deal with complications caused by her brother George.

Even The Hungry Caterpillar exhibits the 'bad' personality trait of greed, and suffers a tummy ache as a result. Even The Teletubbies regularly have reasons to say, "Uh oh...!"

Put in the context of humanity's survival, this feature of story makes perfect sense. Of course we've evolved to pay close attention to narratives containing danger – we're more likely to stay alive when warned of threats!

The concerns of modern humans have extended beyond hazards to our physical health. Today, we're just as concerned about our *mental* health, our relationships, and our environment. Stories have thereby evolved to explore these issues too.

Often, these threats will appear in combination. A character who escapes a flesh-eating giant after nabbing their golden goose is saving his own skin whilst also ensuring the prosperity of his household. A character who overcomes the lure of a vampire is saving both her life and her freedom from oppression. A character who regains the love of his father while beating back an intergalactic dictator is saving the lives of *millions* while strengthening the emotional bonds of family.

Of course, not all stories end happily. For some characters, the Bad Things escalate until there's no way out but death. But it's not the fictional characters who need to learn the survival lessons – it's us, the living, breathing audiences. We're the ones who increase our chances of escaping tragedy by recognising how to avoid similar mistakes in our own lives.

All of which brings us to the *next* vital component...

M for 'Message'

A Bad Thing on its own would be useless. We *know* the world is full of poverty, prejudice, and peril – no-one needs to teach us that. We learn this very the first moment we want something we can't have, find someone who rubs us the wrong way (or vice versa), trip and graze our knee, or any number of other common experiences of childhood.

Stories aided humanity's survival not just because they warned us about the Bad, but because they *helped us deal with it*. In earliest times, that likely meant dealing with starvation by sharing the best sources of food, avoiding pain and suffering by providing examples of how to defend against them, or dealing with competitors for resources by suggesting ways to co-operate with, coerce, or crush them.

M could also be said to stand for 'Moral'. This is the word we often give to the survival component of fairy tales – e.g. "Don't talk to strangers," "Treat others how you wish to be treated," "Don't judge a beast by its horns," etc. But most stories, especially modern stories, have more intricate Messages at their heart. The globally bestselling *Harry Potter*, for example, tackles themes of tolerance, resilience, and companionship – all in book one, before exploring them from a myriad more angles as the series progresses.

In these cases, survival is less about staying alive and more about learning to *thrive*. Prejudice, cowardice, and loneliness *can* be deadly, but individuals and communities alike are far more likely to live happily and peaceably when they work together and encourage one another.

But receiving advice on how to deal with life's challenges is still only two thirds of story. Would Harry's adventures be as enjoyable if he began the series as a wizarding expert, unphased by any of the threats thrown at him, and with an uncanny ability to quickly ascertain who the real villains were and what they were up to?

What if he was *Sherlock Potter?*

E is for 'Empathy'

A 'Sherlock Potter' story might be exciting, and hold one's attention for a time – especially a young reader with a thirst for adventure. But we propose that it could never become a widespread favourite – because few of us could relate to a character who knows everything already, feels no fear, and doesn't struggle at all.

It's hard to present an argument against this point because, as with Bad Things, there aren't many (if any) popular stories *without* at least one main character we can empathise with. The very idea of an indefatigable, undefeatable character actually negates the concept of the Bad Thing. That's why even superheroes have kryptonite, the inability to be in two places at the same time, or friends with *no* superpowers but a knack for getting kidnapped: we *can* all identify with not always feeling our best, having to juggle conflicting priorities, and wanting to protect our nearest and dearest.

Again, from the perspective of humanity's survival, this necessity for us to empathise with the main character(s) makes sense. When deciding whether to give our attention to a story, we're looking to see if it will help *us* to survive. If there's no-one like us with a key decisive role in the tale, what could *we* possibly learn from it?

This is undoubtedly why many of the most successful children's stories feature child/young protagonists – and that's as true for folk and fairy tales as it is for modern bestsellers.

But what about ol' Sherlock *Holmes*? Do we need Empathy less as we age?

Look at virtually any original Sherlock Holmes tale, though, and you'll find yourself looking through the eyes of a *very* empathetic character. Sir Arthur Conan Doyle chose to relate Sherlock's sleuthing through the eyes of a very ordinarily-minded mortal: Dr John Watson.

Watson, like us, is typically baffled by each new mystery – and then astounded by Sherlock's brilliance in solving it. Watson often still plays a key role: he regularly uncovers information for Sherlock that turns out to be an important piece to the puzzle. But Watson's main reason for being there is to ensure that there's someone in the story with whom we *can* identify. Someone who gives Sherlock an excuse to explain his deductions, thus allowing us to learn alongside the good doctor. The importance of Watson's relatable qualities can be measured by the fact that Sherlock's only cases *not* narrated by him are contained within Sir Arthur's final Sherlock collection, which is almost universally judged as inferior.

So perhaps a 'Sherlock Potter' series *could* be a success after all, if told from the perspective of a Dr Ron Weasley...?

The Love of a Good Journey

When young learners first begin to pick up on the usefulness of stories, it manifests as enjoyment. In the past, this 'fun factor' has led some to the misconception that fiction is nothing but entertainment. But working on that principle, you'd have to dismiss other human pursuits as 'nothing but entertainment' too – such as *walking*.

Walking upright has been the natural mode of transport for all humans with the ability to do so for at least 2 million years – yet few toddlers manage it today without the encouragement and praise of an adult. Since an adult can't exactly walk *for* a child, the 'fun factor' of encouragement becomes the first and most important element for teaching them the act of walking.

Consequently, those first few steps often produce the same level of elation one might feel when listening to a favourite piece of music, hearing a hilarious joke, or enjoying a good story.

After a while, though, the vast majority of walkers come to perceive their ability as primarily mechanical, maybe even automatic – a means to an end. A fair few even choose to avoid it where possible. We almost all forget the thrill of those first steps; we forget to see through the toddler's eyes.

But some choose to take up walking recreationally. Research suggests that regularly walking for pleasure leads to improvements in both physical and *mental* health. If you tell a recreational walker that their hobby is good for their survival, you're very unlikely to put them off. It's more likely that you'll stoke their passion yet further.

We believe the same is true for reading. If the current trends (revealed in our **Introduction**) continue, the vast majority of *readers* will mainly perceive the ability to read as primarily mechanical – a means to an end. An increasing number may even choose to avoid it where possible.

But for those who take up reading recreationally, they'll receive the marvellous improvements in physical and mental health discussed in our **Introduction**. And if you tell a recreational reader that their hobby is good for their survival, you're highly unlikely to put them off. More likely you'll stoke that passion yet further. As Terry Pratchet is recorded to have said, "Fantasy is an exercise bicycle for the mind. It might not take you anywhere, but it tones up the muscles that can."

So isn't it time we do for reading what we do for walking, and emphasise the 'fun factor' as the *first and most important element* of teaching the act of reading?

Chapter 4:
Reaching the Reluctant Reader

All the stories included in this book for you to share with your learners have been selected with our 'revised' B-M-E initialism in mind – meaning they should appeal to those primal survival mechanisms in your learners' brains, the 'neurological hooks' of good stories. This will then manifest as engagement, interest, and *enjoyment*.

But for those educators whose own classroom experience has hitherto suggested their learners may struggle to engage with the approach taken in this book, this chapter aims to allay such concerns. If you're interested in the mechanics of this approach, you'll enjoy this chapter too.

Reading for Pleasure and Vocabulary

If you flick ahead to any of the stories in this book, you may glimpse words that you wouldn't ordinarily expect to use around your learners, for fear that they'll have no idea what you mean – and lose interest as a result. Even the stories in **Volume A**, which you'll find us recommending for the youngest learners at primary level, contain some rather rich vocabulary – such as "extinct", "cinders", "haste", and "wit".

The evidence clearly suggests that prolific readers have richer vocabularies (see Ros Wilson's **Foreword** to this book) – so shouldn't we first spark our learners' passion for reading before introducing such high-level vocab? If we start using those less common words from the outset, aren't we at risk of creating a language barrier between your learners and the neurological hooks in these tales?

To allay your concerns, the stories in this book have been written using a methodology Chip developed early in his storytelling career alongside fellow storyteller Amy Scott Robinson (whose poem '**Through the Forest**' also features in this book). They dubbed this method, '**Bigging It Up**'.

Chip and Amy had been invited to tell Ancient Greek legends to a large group of learners aged 7 and 8 at a school in London. Hoping to avoid boring their audience, they diligently searched for a legend that few learners at that level would know, and eventually settled upon the legend of Meleager.

In the middle of this story, the heroes hunt a giant wild boar. As Amy and Chip recounted this scene, their language was escalating – partly from the excitement of the action, but also from a desire to avoid repetition and, again, boring their audience.

As a result, by the time the boar was slain, most synonyms for "cried", "bellowed", "roared" etc had been exhausted – and so Chip declared to the youngsters that "the monster *vociferated!*"

To the surprise of both the storytellers, let alone the observing teachers, not a child batted an eyelid. No-one raised their hand to ask what "vociferated" meant, and no whispers of "Huh?" were heard.

On the contrary, when Amy and Chip led a writing workshop later that morning, several learners chose to *use* that word – and they were clearly using it correctly. They only had one question: "How do you spell 'vociferated'?"

This proved to Amy and Chip that, **once they are hooked into a story, it's possible to raise the level of a learner's comprehension very swiftly indeed** – *even within the same story.*

And so the concept of **'Bigging It Up'** was born: beginning a telling using language that's easy to grasp with the 'lowest common denominator' in terms of vocabulary. Once you have ensured their engagement with (and enjoyment of) the story, you can then gradually raise the richness of your words as the story goes on.

You'll find that these new words stick in your learners' awareness much longer – and much more *accurately* – than if they had needed to turn to a dictionary or put their hand up for a definition. That's almost certainly because this process follows exactly the same mechanism by which we learn our first language.

When you first come into the world, everything you see is a blurry blob. As time passes, you soon recognise that one or more blobs tend to bring sustenance, safety, and/or affection with them. As *more* time passes, you notice that, when those particular blobs are around, there are specific sounds associated with them – e.g. "Mum", "Dad", "Nanna", etc. And when you eventually replicate those sounds, you discover that you can summon one of those blobs and have your needs delivered.

In other words, first we *experience* the world, then we learn to *label* it.

'Bigging It Up' works the same way. When you read for your learners that there are "thick and twisty plants covering the bumpy ground", they can all easily imagine the scene. So when you later read about "the thick and twisty plants *blanketing* the bumpy ground", your learners already know what to imagine – and the new label just sticks on top, without need for explanation. Later, when you return to that location in the tale and remind your learners of the "dense and tangled" plants, those words will also naturally attach to their existing understanding of the scene.

So you needn't be concerned that the language used in these stories will inhibit your learners' engagement. Instead, you can expect to see your learners' vocabularies expand.

Reading for Pleasure and Comprehension

For similar reasons, you needn't fear that your learners will struggle with the *concepts* in the stories in this book – even though *the very first story* (tried and tested on learners with a concentration age as young as 3) contains some of that anthropological understanding we looked at in **Chapter 2**!

Again, once the interest of your learners has been sparked using the natural hooks of a story's B-M-E, you'll notice huge gains in their abilities to comprehend and concentrate upon the content of that tale.

And let's not forget: comprehension is a form of critical thinking – i.e. using what you have in front of you to form your own ideas. As we *also* explored in **Chapter 2**, the development of storytelling resulted in humanity strengthening its aptitude for critical thinking, which subsequently improved its use more generally. You'll witness this with your learners too: sharpen their minds with stories, and you'll have them cutting more competently through the challenges of the *real* world.

Reading for Pleasure and *Reading*

One of the biggest obstacles that educators share with us, though, is their learners' inability to sit and listen to a story for more than one chapter – or, in some cases, little more than ten minutes. But given everything we've claimed in this book so far, shouldn't all learners be sucked into *any* story, whatever their interests, and whatever the length?

Let us return for a moment to the walking analogy from **Chapter 3**. After a child has taken their first steps, and shown more than once that they can confidently walk from one side of a room to the other, would you recommend taking them for a multi-stage trek across town as soon as possible?

Were anyone to do this, the chances are great that the child would have a higher-than-average number of falls, and also tire far faster. While they may have mastered the mechanics of walking, they've yet to build their walking *stamina*. Moreover, they've yet to understand the full *potential* of walking – i.e. independence, rather than simply approaching nearby people and objects – and there's a danger such a trek would put them off.

And yet, this analogy can be applied to how many modern curricula are designed. Young learners are taught their phonics (their 'first steps') in books that rarely contain any B-M-E, and often don't have any narrative at all. This may be because stories are seen as the reading equivalent of 'independence' in walking (i.e. the ultimate goal). Hence, at this stage, it's considered better to set that aside for a while – the focus is first on the mechanics.

After phonics, most young learners are moved onto picture books. Quite a few of these *do* contain some B-M-E – but many if not more present simple and/or silly poems. These lack narrative, let alone story. This can certainly make books fun, and therefore less off-putting, giving learners their chance to 'confidently walk from one side of a room to the other'. But without a sustained and developing exploration of B-M-E, they still aren't given much chance to grasp that 'independence'...

The next stage, though, is often to present young learners with a chapter book, usually with far fewer (if any) illustrations.

In other words, those learners are expected to go from the reading equivalent of walking across a room straight to trekking across a town.

The missing stage, were they learning to walk, would be extended periods of playful pattering through indoor spaces, gardens, and parks. Toddlers are carefully transported to these places by their grown-ups, and gradually build their stamina for longer-range journeys within *fun, safe environments* – where occasional stumbles won't overly hold them back.

In the world of reading, this stage is the *short story*: longer than a picture book, shorter than a chapter book, yet abundant in the structure of B-M-E. Short stories help learners to experience the full power of B-M-E, without presenting them with a long journey for which they're not quite ready. And because short stories aren't split into chapters, the neurological hooks offered by B-M-E tend to arrive far sooner. This allows learners to develop their natural grasp of reading for pleasure more quickly, as well as the stamina for sticking with it.

So of course, that's exactly what you'll find in this book: a selection of fun but *short* stories, each awash with B-M-E.

Reading for Pleasure and Learning

Based on everything we've explored so far in this book, what do you feel should be your first priority when deciding the order in which you teach literacy to your learners? Phonics, comprehension, or reading for pleasure?

Admittedly, reading for pleasure is a relatively recent addition to national curricula, especially here in the UK. But flip your literacy teaching around to nurture the love of reading (and stories) first, and you'll find yourself teaching engaged, capable learners who are *eager* to pick up books and master the mechanics of reading.

By now, though, you may also be cottoning on to the full potential of storytelling as a teaching tool. As mentioned earlier, numerous teachers have noticed their learners make great strides in a *wide* variety of subjects after storytelling interventions. This common anecdotal evidence is backed up by the UCL Institute of Education's finding that learners who read for pleasure are regularly also the highest achievers in non-literary subjects – including Maths.

In some subjects, this may be connected to the fact-absorbing state that our minds enter when presented with a tale saturated in B-M-E. In others, it may be more due to the exponential enhancement to critical thinking that comes from enjoying story after story after story. Most often, it's likely to be a combination of both.

So in this light, what do you feel should be your priority when deciding the order of *all your subjects* for a week? You can probably guess at *our* answer…

Begin every week (if not every *day*) with a focus on reading for pleasure, and you'll move into other subjects with engaged, capable learners – who are *eager* to learn.

Reading for Pleasure and… *Reading for Pleasure*

To end this chapter, we just want to call back to mind the examples we shared from our own experiences back in **Chapter 2**. Experiencing the joy of stories was the *only encouragement* those youngsters needed to seek further experiences of a similar kind through *independent reading*.

The lesson plans in this book will help you to ensure that your learners forge lasting connections between the fun you'll share together and the fun abounding in books. Structured lessons like this are better than just open-ended 'reading for pleasure' time – because if your learners aren't used to getting pleasure out of reading, where's their motivation to make the best use of that time?

Moreover, the joy of *shared* reading with your learners is likely to boost their interest in *independent* reading, because it sets up a *presumption* of pleasure. When their friends invite them to share in whatever they've been watching, playing, visiting, etc, your learners are likely to develop the same passions and interests themselves – because a sizeable portion of the pleasure in an activity comes from knowing that those around you have found it fun before.

Reading is the same: the more you share it with them as a pleasurable experience, the more they'll expect the same pleasure when given the opportunity to read on their own.

That's it for the theory – at least for *this* handbook. If you're now desperate to boost the enthusiasm, engagement, and attainment of your learners, and feel confident in your ability to engage them with your reading, feel free to skip straight ahead to **Section 3: Stories & Lessons**.

But if you're unsure of your ability to engage, or ***too*** *confident in your ability to engage* – or if you're curious as to why we've twice now expressed a concern that some might be ***too*** confident – please enjoy some time in **Section 2: Reading Like a Storyteller**...

Section 2:
Reading Like a Storyteller

The word "storyteller" gets bandied about a lot these days. It's been used to describe authors, artists, singers, filmmakers, actors, comedians, even business strategists, as well as people who are just good at reading aloud. So let's start by clarifying that we're using the word in its traditional, *original* meaning here: simply someone who sits or stands across from you and *tells you a story*.

It sounds obvious, but it also sounds insufficient. After all, if a storyteller is anyone who tells a story, is any person sat around a dinner table a storyteller too? Or everyone stood in a pub? Or all those waiting outside the school gates?

The answer, though, is *Yes* – all those individuals *are* storytellers! Sure, there are folks (like our author Chip) who tell stories for a living. But even professionally, the most engaging storytellers are those who recognise that storytelling is, essentially, the art of *connecting with your audience through a story*.

Anyone who tries to make it something more – e.g. a piece of one-person theatre, a performance routine, a display of 'all the voices' they can do – is not storytelling in the original, *traditional* sense. There's a good chance they'll be incorporating *some* elements of traditional storytelling, along with all the aforementioned benefits these bring – but there's just as good a chance that those elements will be overshadowed by other artistic additions, which may replace or even reduce those benefits.

Our aim here is not to suggest that a professional storyteller doesn't have important insights to share – that would be somewhat self-defeating for a book like this! But we do want to emphasise that absolutely *anyone* who receives those insights is perfectly capable of becoming a storyteller themselves.

Without question, that includes you. So continue through this section for insights into enhancing *your* ability to tell engaging stories...

Chapter 5:
This is NOT a Performance

Chip, the storyteller on the team writing this book, has told stories on many stages – across the UK and across the world. But he never trained as an actor, never went to drama school, and wouldn't describe what he does on stage as 'acting'. It's true that he often deploys many of the tools in an actor's arsenal, including vocal expression, puppetry and ventriloquism, costume, and occasionally (rarely...) a scripted line or two. But he always does something very few actors do:

He lets the audience meet *him* onstage.

After one of Chip's performances at the Edinburgh Fringe Festival, his storytelling show for children was reviewed by the *Primary Times*. One line of praise from the reviewer has been cherished by Chip ever since:

"It felt more like a conversation than a performance."

Tell stories *with* your audience, not *to* them. This isn't just a key skill of good storytelling – it's the *keyring* skill, the one from which all other key skills hang.

It's also the skill most undersung by those who see 'storytelling' as a synonym for 'acting' or 'performing', because, well... everyone can do it! Every time you share an experience from your daily life with someone, hoping to help them understand your emotions and thought-processes... or each time you share some gossip, hoping to provoke a reaction... *That's* the essence of storytelling!

Our purpose here isn't to downplay the skills of actors, stand-up comedians, and other vocal performers. They are often immensely talented individuals who pull off the incredible feat of convincing you that they are someone entirely different to their actual selves. Occasionally, they'll even deploy many of the tools in a *storyteller's* arsenal, such as checking their audience has understood, asking for audience input, and directly quoting others to give a sense of the other personalities involved in the story. And they provide huge value to society through their artistry, be it the relief of entertainment, the insight of social commentary, highlighting injustice, etc.

Plus, of course, traditional storytelling needs a live audience, which can limit its reach. For this reason, *screen* storytelling is commonly among the first and most accessible forms of storytelling a child will encounter, which is immensely invaluable for giving them their first appreciation of story, language, and the sense that they're not alone in the world.

So no, we have nothing against the performing arts – far from it! All we hope to do here is reassure you that **you don't need to be somebody else to be a storyteller – just be yourself. You can already tell engaging stories – you do so whenever you're in conversation with another person.**

We do also want to warn you of a danger, though. As mentioned a couple of times, some people can grow *overly* confident about their storytelling ability. And often this is *coupled* with the perception of storytelling as a performance: the 'storyteller' will take pride in their ability to change their voice, produce sound effects, put on almost elastic facial expressions, etc. This often results in a merry amount of mirth from their listeners.

But while those who perform in this way may well capture the engagement of some (if not all) of their audience, that engagement is unlikely to be with the *story*. Rather, it'll be with the *performer*. And while that's not necessarily a negative, it can stand in the way of the audience receiving the full benefits of story as discussed in **Section 1** – i.e. the increases to their own creativity, critical thinking, and/or understanding of the world.

So how can traditional storytelling help you to strengthen the engagement of your audience with a story?

Don't *Seek* Attention – *Give It*

A performer knows they've done a good job when all eyes and/or ears have been focused on them, and when (if it's a live performance) they receive rapturous applause at the end.

A *storyteller* knows they've done a good job when they detect obvious signs that their audience has engaged with the experience.

Of course, rapturous applause *can* be a sign of engagement. But more often it's the audience's way of praising the performer's talent, rather than reflecting on the value *they themselves* brought to the experience. To understand the difference, consider what it means when there's an *absence* of applause for a performer. That usually suggests that the audience had no interest in or respect for the performer's efforts, much less any impact it may have had on them.

By contrast, a traditional storyteller will feel more certain that their story has been well-received if the audience immediately asks questions about decisions taken by the characters, the truth of the events, where the story came from, etc. All this shows that the audience are considering what the story means *for them*.

This, then, is the way to use the keyring skill of storytelling effectively: be aware of your audience, far more than requiring *them* to be aware of *you*.

One of Chip's favourite personal examples of this is from an occasion when he had been invited to share stories in a school library. Different year groups were brought to him throughout the day – and when the learners aged 10 and 11 arrived, a young lad took one look at Chip and declared, "If it's not football, I'm not interested."

Immediately, the boy's teacher clicked her fingers and demanded that he come and sit by her feet. Forcibly separated from his friends, the boy sat and slumped with the attitude of someone who thinks the world is against them.

So even before Chip had spoken to this audience, this lad had a number of barriers to overcome. By his own admission, he had no interest in the activity on offer. He'd also been reprimanded, so he was in the headspace of someone on the defensive rather than curious. And separated from his friends, he couldn't be affected by their enjoyment.

But Chip also immediately knew something about this lad: he was into football. This indicated he likely enjoyed physical activity, and would probably enjoy stories involving elements of physical prowess and competition.

After a discussion with the group as a whole that suggested their enthusiasm for an adventurous tale, Chip decided to tell an Arthurian legend surrounding the game of jousting. He added plenty of opportunities for the entire audience to move about and imagine themselves in the thick of physical combat. Moreover, he ensured he made eye contact with that lad on several occasions, letting him know the story was being told as much for him as anyone else.

The result? By the end, this young lad who had originally self-declared as "not interested" was joining in with all the actions, gasping at the unexpected twists, and smiling as wide as all his peers by the time the hero triumphed.

This could only have been achieved by Chip focusing on the needs of his audience, rather than sticking to a plan or a script, or prioritising *their* focus on *him*.

Adapting Your Reading

Of course, Chip's profession requires the skill of swiftly adapting his delivery based on the reactions of brand-new audiences. He can also pull a story from his head to match their preferences based on just a short initial discussion, and will adjust the language he uses to ensure he's being understood. When reading aloud, your words and content are proscribed, so you're limited in the use you could make of such a skillset.

But you *won't need* these skills – because, unlike a traditional storyteller, *you* have the luxury of getting to know your learners over time. This allows you to grow an understanding of what works for them – and plan for it.

This doesn't mean choosing only books involving sports of some kind, in order to appease the football fanatics among your learners. Nor must you only pick books about dinosaurs, mermaids, space travel etc. But if, for instance, you're reading an animal story to a group that includes some learners who love getting physically active, why not ask those learners to demonstrate what it might be like to move as those animals? If you're reading a fantasy story to a group including science enthusiasts, why not pause the story to discuss what real-life solutions could let us enjoy the effects of magic spells like levitation, shining a light, etc? And if you're telling *any* story to a group including someone who loves nothing more than drawing, why not give that learner a pencil and paper and ask them to illustrate the story as you read it?

In short, allowing your learners to engage in their own ways will vastly increase the level of their engagement, regardless of the tale.

We All Engage Differently

Just before this book went to print, Chip was invited to share stories with the small group of learners at Hope Tree School in Cambridge, UK, a special school for girls aged 8 to 12 who have "significant barriers to learning and/or gaps in their educational journey." Prior to beginning, he was warned that the learners might be restless, or even get up and leave, due to them typically feeling uncomfortable around strangers. He was also advised not to expect much audience participation.

It's true that this audience was quiet for the first fifteen minutes or so. But by the end of the afternoon, every learner had made at least one vocal contribution, most had joined in with some 'Environment' participation (see the next chapter), and *all* were still there at the end – with bright smiles and keen applause. While one or two learners had needed to get up and move mid-story, they surprised their teachers by always coming back.

One learner's reaction particularly impressed the teachers, though. For the first hour, Bethany (whose name has been shared with permission from her and her mother) was focused almost exclusively on the tablet she held in front of her – though she did occasionally ask a trusted member of staff to vocalise her responses at various moments during Chip's telling.

Then, in the first break between stories, this 12-year-old asked her trusted member of staff to show Chip what she'd been drawing on the tablet – and he couldn't help but gasp...

Cross-reference this incredible portrait with the photo of Chip at the back of this book, and you'll see just how much attention to detail she has shown. Surely Bethany couldn't have been giving any attention to Chip's story if she was busy producing such an intricate work of art?

And yet, she *had* been As mentioned above, there were multiple occasions when Bethany had responded to Chip's telling by making a comment through that trusted member of staff. And what's more, her teachers expressed a level of astonishment at the fact that Bethany in particular had remained present throughout Chip's entire visit. For her, this was a rare occurrence – so she *must* have been actively enjoying the experience.

Bethany's story is a fantastic example of the fact that *we all engage differently*. A storyteller who demands that all eyes look in the same direction could erect a barrier to engagement rather than enable it. Conversely, allowing a learner to relax and enjoy a story in their own way could result in far greater engagement than the learner would be otherwise capable of.

Hundreds of traditional storytellers, including Chip, have shared stories in schools for learners with physical and mental disabilities. Such learners are often incapable of displaying engagement in the ways that most of us are used to, such as eye contact, smiling, or responding to questions. Yet it swiftly becomes clear to the specialists who work with them on a daily basis that these learners most certainly *are* engaging – and often, the attention they receive *from* the storyteller has a profound and positive impact upon them.

But what about the learners who keep turning to chat with their friends during a story, or those disrupt a tale by making sudden sounds to the annoyance and/or amusement of those around them? Are *they* engaging with the tale?

In our experience – and in the experience of every traditional storyteller we know – those learners are always providing some sort of commentary on the story, or contributing their own sound effects, dialogue, gestures, etc. So why would you silence them? That's a clear sign that they're engaged!

Always keep this in mind: every learner will engage differently. Your knowledge of them will help you to determine whether they are displaying their engagement in a manner that's unique to them. This may also help you to consider how you might adapt your future readings in order to increase their levels of engagement further.

The Keyring Skill

Ultimately, then, your success as an oral reader comes down to this: how much agency you give to your listeners over the reading experience (and how much control you can relinquish regarding your own fixed expectations...). And this brings us back to that all-important 'keyring skill' of good storytelling – which, adapted for the purposes of this book, can be rephrased as follows:

Read *with* your learners, not *to* them.

This is the principle from which all other tools of engagement hang. In the next chapter, we'll share some of those tools, focusing on the ones that are simplest for any educator to implement.

But if you don't feel confident or comfortable using any of the techniques in the next chapter, don't worry – the keyring skill is the *only* one you actually *need*.

If you read with *your* learners in mind, we promise that you cannot fail to engage them.

Chapter 6:
Doing All the VOICE

In the last chapter, we cautioned against considering 'a great storyteller' to be someone who can 'do all the voices'. But as a concession to that common line of thought, it does make a memorable acronym for the five simplest key skills to hang from your *keyring* skill: VOICE can stand for...

Vocal Adjustments
Openings
Indication
Conversation
Environment

Before we explore these in more detail, please keep this in mind throughout: **none of these are essential.** Being 'key' means they *can* unlock engagement – but sometimes the keys won't fit. Your learners may not care for any of these techniques – or, as is more often the case, *the story alone will be engaging enough.*

That said, let's share some of the best insights that the world of traditional storytelling can offer those who plan to read aloud for an audience...

Vocal Adjustments

This is something you do all the time, usually without thinking about it. If you're concerned, you lower your pitch; if you're excited, you increase your pace; if you're trying to get someone's attention across a crowded room, you project.

For those on the receiving end, there's an almost universal unconscious understanding of what these Vocal Adjustments mean. Someone speaks to you with a lower pitch than usual? You probably want to know what's wrong. Someone's speaking too fast? You may ask them to slow down so you can understand why they're so excited. A loud voice cuts across a great distance? You may turn to look, checking whether it's your attention they want.

So if all this nuance of language can be transmitted automatically, you can be sure of enhancing your reading by putting just a little thought into it in advance. When reading a passage, consider how it's making *you* feel. How would you adjust your voice if trying to convey that same feeling? Try reading the passage out loud with that same Vocal Adjustment, and you'll share the same emotion with your listeners.

You can apply this approach to characters in a story, too. What emotion is the *character* feeling? How would you adjust *your* voice to convey such a feeling? Read their dialogue with that same Vocal Adjustment, and all your listeners will feel a greater understanding for the character.

Adjusting for emotion is far more powerful than attempting to adjust for gender, accent, species, etc. Yes, those other sorts of vocal adjustments can be fun to listen to. But chances are your listeners won't be drawn further into the *story* when they hear those sorts of vocal techniques. Instead, they'll observe you *performing* those voices, and be impressed (but also distracted) by your talent.

In other words, adjusting your vocals is *not* the same as 'doing all the voices'. The latter makes you the object of attention. Vocal Adjustments designed around *emotion*, by contrast, spark a *creative response within the mind of the listener*, as they imagine how the characters are feeling, or get a better sense of the action taking place.

There is one advantage to changing your voice to match a specific character, though: *clarity*. For stories with a sizeable cast, your listeners may get a quicker idea of who's speaking at any one time if you have a distinct voices for each character. Can you achieve this clarity without drawing attention to yourself as a performer?

Here are our three favourite solutions to this conundrum. First, **don't let the voice differ too much from your own.** Never underestimate the impact a slight change in pitch, speed, or volume can make, especially when combined with consistency. If your listeners hear your voice always rise *slightly* in pitch when you deliver the dialogue of a mouse, for example, they will quickly come to associate that voice with the mouse.

The second solution makes use of the **Indication** skill we'll discuss a little later in the chapter: **change your physical position for each character.** Again, this needn't be anything too complicated; we're not suggesting you scrunch yourself up into as small a space as possible when reading the words of that mouse. You need only sag a little to your right when reading as the mouse, then straighten up to your left when reading as a character replying to that mouse. Consistency is the key: if you're always in the same position whenever you read the mouse's lines, your listeners will always associate that position with that character.

The final solution, though, combines Vocal Adjustment with the **Conversation** skill discussed later this chapter: **ask your listeners how *they* think the character should sound.**

This is an especially engaging option, because it encourages your listeners to invest their imagination in the telling – and remember that keyring skill: read *with* your learners, not *to* them. Not only will this option help your listeners distinguish between characters, but it will help them to care more about the story too.

Openings

If you're confident that your listeners will predict the next word, then preceding it with the inflexion of a question mark, along with a slight pause, can prompt them to say it for (or with) you.

Doing this gives you an opportunity to confirm the engagement of your listeners – but not just for you. When they hear *themselves* providing the right response, they'll be recognising their *own* engagement. **Essentially, this will give rise to a 'feedback loop': hearing themselves (and others) engaging with the tale will encourage them to engage even more.**

Once your learners are familiar with your use of this technique, though, it can be fun to play around with it, and provide an Opening when, in fact, the next word is *not* what you'd expect. The fact that they still make an attempt is proof of their engagement – but the gasp, laughter, or other sounds of surprise or delight will again create that feedback loop for their own engagement.

Be careful not to *overuse* this technique, though. A reading with too many Openings can become tedious, especially if the listeners haven't yet become acquainted enough with the tale to make an educated guess at what's coming – or if they're never allowed to be right.

In the stories in this book (and also the Educator Editions of Chip and Korky's *Fables & Fairy Tales* series published by Epic Tales), we've included a clue in the punctuation to let you know the best moments to use an Opening. If you haven't quite reached the end of a sentence or a paragraph, but you find yourself coming across an ellipsis (...) followed by a question mark, that's an...?

Opening – exactly.

In all instances where we suggest Openings, give it a try. We're confident that your learners will respond if they're able to do so.

Indication

Let's say you're listening to someone telling a story about a spider. They say, "This story is about a very small creature..." – and, at the same time, hold out a closed hand that *isn't quite* a fist. They look at their hand, and add, "...who was actually..."

Slowly, they open their fingers, palm towards the ceiling.

"...a *spider*," they finish.

In that moment, what are you imagining to be in their hand?

Even without the presence of an actual arachnid, the storyteller's gesture has guided your imagination to create an *Indication* of one. And as you'll find us saying again and again later in this book, if your listeners are creating, they're *investing in the experience of your story* – which is the very definition of engagement.

Indication works best when it combines three core elements...

1. **a physical gesture** (e.g. a hand held out);

2. **a *suggestion of mass*** (e.g. by not fully closing the hand); and

3. **the teller's *sight line*** (e.g. looking at their hand).

Of these, item 3 is the most important. If you look up as if you're seeing an elephant and declare, "The elephant stood up!" then your audience will be more convinced that you are Indicating an elephant standing up. That, in turn, will encourage *them* to envision the same – even though you haven't used a physical gesture, nor given any suggestion of mass.

Item 2 is perhaps the most subtle of the ingredients, but a powerful one nonetheless. If you hold up a completely closed fist, how could anyone imagine a spider actually waiting safely in your palm for your revelation? How could they believe you're holding an apple, a sword, a rope, or anything else?

It is also under this heading that we would include the use of pictures, props, puppets, or even volunteers. In all these cases, you can only ever give an Indication of what's happening in the story, because the world of the story is ultimately and entirely in the heads of your listeners. Such tools can be useful in specific situations – for example, if you're about to tell a story about a camel to a group of learners who may not know what a camel is, showing a picture of a camel before you begin will help them imagine the story.

Or if it's important that a character from the beginning isn't forgotten, even though they're barely mentioned during the middle, 'clothing' a member of your audience to be an Indication of that character – be it with items of costume, a physical position, or just a comment – can ensure that character is kept in mind.

Never forget, though, that the goal is always to let your audience focus mainly on the story playing out *inside their minds*, rather than the world around them – so the more you require them to invest their imagination, the more they'll remain engaged with the story.

Conversation

Ah, we're back to Chip's favourite review comment again! (See above, page 29.) As you go through the story, invite your listeners to comment on it, say what *they* think is about to happen, what *they* would do in a similar situation, etc. There is quite simply no better method of confirming and compounding the engagement of your audience.

Conversation needn't just be about the story, either. It can also cover the *telling* of the story. As already mentioned, you can ask your listeners to suggest how a character might sound. You can ask them how they think the *environment* should sound. You could even ask them if there's anything they'd like to do to feel more involved in the story, such as turning up the lights so they can see you more easily – or turning them *down* for a *spooky* story…

There are two important factors to consider when using this key skill. The first is to avoid giving your audience any suggestion of *control* over the story. For example, instead of asking, "What happens next?", your question should be, "What *do you think* will happen next?" By doing so, you'll avoid the potential of engagement-busting disappointment when you read on to reveal an action that entirely contradicts your listener's suggestion. You'll also avoid any sense of competition between the ideas of your listeners. If all you invited was their *thoughts*, you can legitimately move on with the words, "Shall we find out?"

> **Top Telling Tip:** When canvassing your audience for their ideas on a character's thoughts, feelings, actions, etc, respond to every suggestion with enthusiasm, perhaps exploring it in more detail. For example, if a learner suggests that a character should run away, you could respond with, "Yes! Then maybe she'll get to stay out of trouble! I think that's probably what I would try to do, even if it would be hard."
>
> This way, your learners will grow in confidence from sensing that their ideas are valuable and encouraged. You may even find, as others have, that this increased confidence in hand-raising then starts to manifest in other subjects too, such as when those learners need assistance in maths…

The second factor to consider is knowing when to move on. Don't lose sight of the fact that you're telling a story – and you need time to finish it!

> **Top Telling Tip:** When a moment of conversation leads to multiple hands being raised by learners keen to comment, one of Chip's favourite ways to move on is to acknowledge all of those hands with a wide gesture whilst saying, "*Lots* of different ideas were going through [the character's] head – but in the end, this is what [they] did…"
>
> Again, such a technique indicates that every idea has value, even if it goes unheard. And if you're reading to your learners as regularly as you should, and making this technique a big part of your reading style, each child will soon have their chance to speak out.

Conversation may be the most powerful key skill on your keyring. To help you use it, you'll find questions *written into* most of the stories within this book, as well as those in Chip and Korky's *Fables & Fairy Tales* series. When you come to these questions, take time to gather some responses from your learners.

Environment

The final key skill we'll share with you here is the easiest form of audience participation: inviting your listeners to create the *story Environment* with you.

There is in fact an entire lesson inspired by this key skill early in the next Section (**Lesson A2: The Story Cave**), but we don't just mean the look and/or feel of the location where you're sharing your stories. A big part of the Environment is in fact *your learners themselves* – so why not use them?

For example, you read that a wind is blowing through the trees. Why not invite your learners to make the sound of that breeze? By contributing to the atmosphere of the story, they'll feel further invested in it. Don't worry about silencing them afterwards, either – just continue to read, raising your voice ever so slightly *if needed*, and you'll soon find your learners quietening down naturally in order to discover the action that takes place in the setting they've helped to establish.

Letting learners join in with repeated phrases can also add to the story Environment. When they join in with a refrain, they get that 'feedback loop' on their engagement again: they hear that they've learned a piece of the story, confirming that they paid some attention – and so they pay even more.

Refrains work even better when combined with a physical gesture. This doesn't have to be huge or intricate. For example, when telling the stories of '**Huh**' that you'll find in this book, Chip usually opens and closes his hands four times in quick succession whenever he speaks the words, "*Forty thousand years!*" Doing so draws attention to this important refrain, and soon has everyone in the room reciting it with him. And if you visit YouTube and search for "Chip and Amy Through the Forest", you should find the very simple actions these storytellers crafted to encourage audience participation in Amy Scott Robinson's poem '**Through The Forest**', also included in this book (in **Story Volume A**) for you to share with your learners.

One of the reasons refrains are a great form of Environment participation is because you will likely find you don't have to invite your learners to join in. Indeed, issuing an invitation can sometimes *break* engagement, because you're taking your learners out of the world of the story and back into the classroom, asking them to consider an instruction from their educator.

When you first encounter the refrain, boldly perform your action. The second time, add a slight Opening to the start of it. Do this again for your third time, and many of your learners will begin to join in. From that point on, you'll probably find most if not all are eagerly participating.

In this book, and in the Educator Editions of Chip and Korky's *Fables & Fairy Tales* series, you'll occasionally come across phrases printed in **<u>bold and underlined text</u>**. These are our suggestions for when your learners could join in with you – be it by saying the words along with you, joining in with a repeated action, or both. Before reading the story to your learners, take some time to plan and consider an action that will be appropriate, easy, and comfortable to repeat, so you're ready when it comes up in the reading.

Never Forget Your Keyring

We're fairly confident that all the key storytelling techniques described here will be easy for you to deploy in your own reading – and we hope you are too.

But always keep in mind that each of these skills is *optional*. Some won't fit in every story, and some won't fit with every *audience*. As always, the *keyring* rule is**...?**

Read *with* your learners, not *to* them. Select your key skills based on your knowledge of what is likely to work with *your* learners.

Always hold onto that thought, and it won't be long before, first, you hear your learners describe you as "the best storyteller ever...!"

...and, second, you believe them.

Section 3: Stories and Lessons

How to Use This Section

Time for the exciting bit! As mentioned at the start (and in the blurb), this book has been designed so that, right now, you can carry it into a room with your learners, turn to a title, and engage them in a wondrous tale. And on the pages immediately after each tale, you'll find one or two ready-to-go lesson plans to stoke the fire of enthusiasm for reading among your learners.

That said, if you *can* curb your enthusiasm just a short while longer, these next few pages contain some guidance and suggestions to help you get the *best* out of the stories and lessons to follow…

"Which Materials For *My* Learners?"

This section is split into two Volumes, each with its own selection of stories and associated lessons: **Universal** and **Upper**.

We offer two corresponding pathways through this book. The **Universal Pathway** only uses materials from Volume A, and is suitable for learners with a concentration span of 20–40 minutes.

The **Upper Pathway** uses materials from *both* Volumes, and is suitable for concentration spans 40+ minutes.

If you're using this book in a school, you may find it makes sense for those teaching learners aged 5–7 to use the Universal Pathway, and those teaching ages 7+ to use the Upper Pathway. But note that, when suggesting the suitability of each Pathway, we focused on 'concentration span' rather than age or educational stage.

This is because *most* learners will have developed the ability to concentrate for more than 40 minutes by the physical age of 7, but this can be affected by a huge range of factors – not least the amount of physical activity they've been able to enjoy.[1] If anything has inhibited a learner's capacity for concentration, they may be better beginning on the Universal Pathway regardless of their age.

That said, it's also entirely possible for learners as young as 5 to keenly concentrate on the stories and lessons in Volume B – especially if they've already completed the Universal Pathway. If you sense they have an appetite for exploring more advanced echelons of reading, by all means share the materials in Volume B with them!

---

1 Heaps of studies have shown that movement stimulates brain development, and that younger learners especially need regular physical activity to support the vital early stages of brain growth – including their ability to concentrate! If you're interested in exploring this topic further, we recommend Jensen, *Teaching with the Brain in Mind*, 2005 (2nd edition).

At this point, it's worth repeating what we wrote in the Introduction: **reading for pleasure isn't a gradable skill – it's a mindset that can be cultivated at any age.** Provided your learner(s) fall within the guidelines for concentration outlined on the previous page, you need never worry about concepts going over their heads – but equally, you need never fear them feeling like the 'work' is beneath them.

"How Long Will I Need?"

Including your readings of the stories, you should expect lessons in the Universal Pathway to take 45 minutes to an hour, and those in the Upper Pathway to take at least an hour.

Volume A has ten lessons and Volume B has five. However, three are marked with this sign:

These lessons are *Recyclable* – you can adapt them for future stories, such as the other stories in this book. **You could even use them for books in your chosen phonics scheme, your class reads, and (some) non-fiction texts (e.g. the *Horrible Histories* series) to heighten interest in those titles too.** At the end of this book, you'll find adaptable blank planning sheets for each Recyclable lesson.

Including the Recyclable lessons, each Pathway (described on the page overleaf) has a total of 15 lessons – so if you do two or three lessons per week, you can complete either Pathway in a single term.

"When Can/Should/*Will* I Fit These In?"

You *can* fit them in whenever, so you might be tempted to save them as an end-of-day treat (for *you* as much as your learners!). After all, reading for pleasure is a recent addition to the curriculum, so it makes sense to try and shoehorn it into the end of each day, right? After the Maths, Science, and other subjects that have been our priorities since the dawn of state education? And if that means you don't have time for it after all, so be it...

But as we explored in Section 1, reading for pleasure is what will motivate your learners to pick up books – *all* books, be it phonics books, class reads, and non-fiction – so we strongly recommend you put these lessons at the *front* of your timetable.

If you start on the first morning of the week, for example, you'll begin that week with highly motivated learners. Do a second of these lessons on the third or fourth morning, and you'll rekindle that motivation before it flags. For those weeks when you need do a third, try it on the week's final morning, to give your learners a burst of motivation that could well calm the pre-weekend chaos.

If you timetable the lessons this way, you *will* find it easy to fit them in – because the enthusiasm, concentration, and curiosity that B-M-E inspires in your learners will carry over into their other learning, helping them to grasp things faster and achieve more in less time. (Check Chapter 3 if you missed the lowdown on what B-M-E stand for.)

And once you're done with the stories in this book, don't forget to use the Recyclable lessons on future books. We recommend fiction with themes related to other topics in your curriculum – moments in History, places in Geography, discoveries in Science, etc. Put related fiction like this at the start of the week, and the B-M-E in those tales will empower your learners in those other subjects too.

The Universal Pathway (Concentration Span 20–40min)

Note that, although we say these materials are suitable for a concentration span of 20+ minutes, we wouldn't recommend diving into them on any child's first ever day of school. Ideally, you learners should first have had some time to settle into your learning culture, and to become familiar with the concept of 'story time'. For at least their first ever term of school, you can heighten their excitement for reading just by sharing a few favourite picture books with them (*yours* as well as theirs) and using as many VOICE techniques as you can.

Beyond that, the Universal Pathway is simple: just read through Volume A in order, remembering to reuse the Recyclable lessons. For clarity, the Universal Pathway looks like this:

READ:	'Huh'
LESSON A1:	The Most Important Invention Ever! (I)
LESSON A2:	Building a Story Cave
READ:	'Through the Forest'
LESSON A3:	Fun on the Page
LESSON A4:	Story Links (I)
READ:	'One Lost Slipper'
LESSON A5:	Where Stories Come From (I)
LESSON R1:	Fun on the Page (Recyclable)
LESSON A6:	What a Story Needs
READ:	'Tiger's Terror'
LESSON A7:	Where Stories Come From (II)
LESSON R1:	Fun on the Page (Recyclable)
LESSON R2:	What a Story Needs (Recyclable)
LESSON A8:	Story Links (II)
READ:	'The REAL King of the Jungle'
LESSON A9:	What's Going to Happen? (I)
LESSON R1:	Fun on the Page (Recyclable)
LESSON R2:	What a Story Needs (Recylable)
LESSON A10:	What's Going to Happen? (II)

The Upper Pathway
(Concentration Span 40min+)

If you're teaching learners who have already enjoyed the Universal Pathway earlier in their schooling, you can simply go through the stories and lessons in Volume B in order. That said, depending on how much time has passed since they last heard them, you may want to re-read the stories from Volume A that are used in Volume B's lessons. And of course, *don't forget to use the Recyclable lessons after each new story*.

If *none* of your learners have experienced the materials before, though, there's still no need to take them through the entire Universal Pathway first. Instead, follow this order:

READ:	'Huh'
LESSON A1:	The Most Important Invention Ever! (I)
READ:	'Huh, Part 2'
LESSON B1:	The Most Important Invention Ever! (II)
READ:	'One Lost Slipper'
LESSON A5:	Where Stories Come From (I)
LESSON A6:	What a Story Needs
LESSON B2:	We Need Stories
READ:	'The Mountain Inside a Molehill'
LESSON B3:	Where Stories Come From (III)
LESSON R1:	Fun on the Page (Recyclable)
LESSON R2:	What a Story Needs (Recyclable)
LESSON R3:	We Need Stories (Recyclable)
READ:	'The Shapeshifter'
LESSON B4:	Where Stories Come From (IV)
LESSON R1:	Fun on the Page (Recyclable)
LESSON R2:	What a Story Needs (Recylable)
LESSON R3:	We Need Stories (Recyclable)
READ:	'Seething at the Sea'
LESSON B5:	Stories Need *Us*...
LESSON A10:	What's Going to Happen? (II)

Delivering the Lessons

All these lessons follow a structure that will hopefully be recognisable to most teachers in the UK, and which contains several features tested and proven to help learners get the most out of the activities...

Starter Activity
This introductory activity eases your learners into the right mindset for the main activities, preparing them for the gains in knowledge, skill, and/or understanding to come.

Main Activity
Here's where the bulk of the learning takes place. If a story forms part of the lesson, this is where it will be read.

Independent Activity
This gives your learners the chance to consolidate the knowledge, skill, and/or understanding they picked up during the main activity.

Note that 'independent activity' does not mean each learner needs to work on their own. **We highly recommend letting your learners choose whether they work individually, in pairs, or in small groups.** Some learners thrive best on their own, but others thrive when given the opportunity to bounce ideas off their peers.

Plenary
To end each lesson, you'll bring the learners all back together to share something from their independent work, and/or discuss all that's taken place within the lesson.

Never skip this part – even if you lose track of time and the bell goes, it's important to spend *at least a minute* on the plenary activity. Since these stories and lessons are all designed to produce feelings of pleasure among your learners, you may be surprised by how willing they'll be to forgo some of their break in order to complete the lesson as planned.

For Your Eyes Only

IMPORTANT: Do *not* announce the Learning Outcome! This, together with the Success Criteria, is given to help *you* understand what's going on, not your learners.

Although letting your learners know an intended Learning Outcome can sometimes help them focus, with *these* lessons it is more likely to have an adverse effect. This is because announcing a Learning Outcome effectively states, "This is a lesson" – and unless your learners expect nothing but pleasure from a lesson, that could set up an instinctive barrier to any enjoyment you hope to engender.

If this makes you nervous, remember that, in the very first two chapters of this book (or, if you haven't enjoyed Section 1 yet, read it *now!*), we shared incontrovertible proof that, where stories are involved, learning happens *naturally*, without any need to state a Learning Outcome.

For similar reasons, we also caution you not to announce these lessons as 'story time', 'reading time', etc. If a learner expects to take no pleasure from reading, that very expectation will inhibit their ability to do so.

Rather, dive straight in with the Starter Activity, and continue from there. If your learners are so used to being given Learning Outcomes and/or Success Criteria that they ask for them, simply say, "I'm not sure yet. Let's see, shall we?" – and you'll instil an atmosphere of intrigue and play.

The Lesson Space

The best space for reading these stories is one without tables, and ideally without chairs either. Some older learners feel genuinely uncomfortable sitting on a carpet; if so, allowing them to lie on their sides is better than requiring them to slouch on chairs.

If moving your tables and chairs out of the way is impossible, try to find another space where sitting on the floor is both possible and comfortable. If you really must use an environment where tables will be in the way, that's fine – but be aware that you'll need to put extra energy into ensuring the lesson looks *nothing like* a lesson, so your learners can be more open to the possibility of relaxing and enjoying the activity.

When sharing the stories, have your learners sit so they are all facing you *and only you*. While 'story circles' are a common idea, they're actually conducive to *distraction* rather than engagement – they make it too easy for your learners to focus on each other rather than you and the story. Moreover, you'll find it harder to give your attention to all your learners at once, since some will always be slightly outside your natural field of vision – and remember: paying attention to your learners is the Keychain Skill…

What to Expect Now

In just a few pages, you'll find the first story to share with your learners. Read it through in your planning time first, though, so you can give thought to where and how you'll employ your VOICE.

Immediately after the story is the first lesson plan. Beyond that, you'll find a segment entitled **Behind the Scenes** – there we go into a bit more detail about what you're doing and why. *Be sure to read this before using the plan* – the more you understand what's going on, the easier you'll find it to adapt the lesson to your unique group of learners.

So that's it! You're all set! When you're ready, turn the page to enter Volume A…

…and Happy Reading!

Huh

Based on true archaeological findings
Written by Chip Colquhoun
Illustrated by Korky Paul

What I'm about to share with you is the most amazing story you will ever hear. It may not be your *favourite* story ever, but it really is amazing, it really is important, and it really *is*...

...true.

In fact, it's so amazing, so important, *and* so true, I probably shouldn't share it with you – *unless* you can show me that you deserve to hear it. I need to know that your brains are good at thinking. So here's what we'll do. Think for a moment: How long ago do you think people started sharing stories?

No need to answer out loud: just hold your answer inside your head for a moment. How long ago do you think people started sharing stories? And if your answer is *bigger* than one hundred years, hold your hand up.

Now, before I let you know the right answer, I should just tell you: holding your hand up *now* is like saying that storytelling is older than *television*.

Does that sound right? If you think Yes, if you think storytelling is *definitely* older than television, hold your hand up.

Well, I can tell you that holding your hand up right now is...

...the *right* answer.

OK, that was quite easy really, wasn't it. So let's make it twice as hard. Hold your hand up if you think storytelling is older than *two* hundred years.

Hmm. Before I tell you the correct answer *this* time, I should just warn you: holding your hand up *now* is like saying that storytelling is older than *most of the schools in the world*. That's because schools only really became popular when they were made free in England just over two hundred years ago. So – if you think storytelling is older than most of the places where storytelling happens today, hold your hand up.

Well now. Holding your hand up *now* is...

...the *correct* answer!

OK, let's see how you do if I make it twice as hard again. Hold your hand up if you think storytelling is older than**...**? *Four* hundred years.

Once again, let me just advise you: holding your hand up *now* is like saying that storytelling is older than *Shakespeare*.

Now, Shakespeare is probably the most famous storyteller in the world. He wrote stories like *Romeo and Juliet* and *A Midsummer Night's Dream*, and his stories have been in books, theatres, films, and even computer games. So if you think storytelling is even older than the most famous storyteller in the world... hold your hand up.

Well. Holding your hand up *this* time is...

...*correct!*

You know, I can tell you're thinking about this really well. I think you can skip right to the higher levels. So I tell you what: hold your hand up if you think storytelling is older than six *thousand* years...

Six thousand is a big number! And let me just advise you: holding your hand up *now* is like saying that storytelling is older than *paper*.

Does that make sense? Could people have shared stories before they had paper to write them on? If you think Yes, hold your hand up.

Ooo. Holding your hand up *now* is *actually*...

...*correct!*

Alright, just one more. Hold your hand up if you think storytelling is older than... *ten thousand years*...

D'you know, I'm a little worried now that you might you just need to hold your hand up every time, and then you'll be *correct* every time. So before I tell you the answer *this* time, there are *two* warnings I have for you.

First, remember: I *did* say this was the *last one*...

...and second, holding your hand up right now is like saying that storytelling is older... than *talking*.

Does that make sense? Could people have told stories *before they could talk?* Remember: even sign language is a way of talking, and sign language was only invented *after* people had said words out loud first. So if you think people were telling stories to each other *even before they could talk*... hold your hand up.

Well. Holding your hand up now is *obviously*...

...correct!

That's right! Scientists believe the oldest story in the world is about as old as **forty thousand years** – and that's a story that was painted on the walls of a cave where people used to live.

Scientists don't really know what that story was about, because there were no words to go with the pictures. But they *think* those pictures tell a story about what those people saw when they went for walks outside their cave.

So now! Because you've done so much good thinking already, I reckon you *do* deserve to hear this amazing, important, and true story. It's the story of one of those people who lived in a cave about **forty thousand years** ago...

Did you know that people used to live in caves around **forty thousand years** ago? Not only that but, in those days, there were lots of different *kinds* of people. There were humans like you and me, but there were other types of people too – like the neanderthals.

Humans and neanderthals were almost exactly the same as each other. Take the human and neanderthal in *this* story. The human's name was Huh, which meant, "Oo, that's interesting." And the neanderthal was called Nuh, which meant, *"Nuffink gits in my way!"*

If you went into a cave and found only one of them, you would probably find it hard to know whose cave you were in, because Huh the human and Nuh the neanderthal *looked* almost exactly the same. They both wore furry capes wrapped around their hairy bodies. They both had big, bulging muscles. They were both dotted all over with mud, because they hadn't invented showers yet.

Only if you stood them next to each other would you notice that Nuh was a little taller than Huh, and Nuh had a slightly bigger head too.

Huh would look all around and say, "Huh," which meant, "Oo, that's interesting."

Nuh would look at himself and say, "Nuh!" – which meant, *"Nuffink gits in my way!"*

Who do you think was cleverest?

Who had some catching up to do?

If you watched only one of them during the day, you would probably find it hard to know who you were following, because Huh and Nuh *behaved* almost exactly the same, too. They both spent the morning sharpening a long wooden stick into a tool for catching food. They both spent the afternoon using that tool to catch a wild pig. They even both spent the evening making a campfire in their cave to cook the pig and eat it.

Only if you sat them next to each other would you notice that Nuh carried a heavier tool, and caught a bigger pig too.

Huh would look at his little pig cooking on the fire and say, "Huh," which meant**…?** "Oo, that's interesting."

Nuh would look at his big pig on the fire and say, "Nuh!" – which meant**…?** *"Nuffink gits in my way!"*

Who do you think would live the longest?

Who had some catching up to do?

If you watched only one of them at night, though, you'd find it *very easy* to know who you were watching. Both Huh and Nuh liked to decorate their caves at night using ash from the fire, but Huh liked to draw *pictures*. He drew pictures of animals he'd seen during the day, pictures of his family and friends, and sometimes pictures of his dreams – like one of his friends with the head of an animal!

Huh would stand back to look at his pictures and say, "Huh," which meant**…?** "Oo, that's interesting."

Nuh, though, would use the ash from the fire to put his handprint on the wall. "My cave!" he would declare, then go back to eating his big pig and say, "Nuh!" – which meant**…?** *"Nuffink gits in my way!"*

Who do you think knew the most important things to do every day?

Who had some catching up to do?

But then, around **forty thousand years** ago, the weather began to change. It began to get cold – *very* cold. The land was covered in thick sheets of ice which didn't melt for ages – and so it became known as an Ice Age. Only a few plants poked through the top of the ice, and many animals died and were never seen again – like the woolly mammoth, the sabre-toothed tiger, and the giant cave lion.

Suddenly, Nuh the neanderthal and his neanderthal friends didn't know what to do. They couldn't find food in the same places, so they grew hungry. They couldn't *catch* food using the same tools as before, so they grew hungrier. And soon, they all went extinct – like the woolly mammoth, the sabre-toothed tiger, and the giant cave lion.

But Huh the human and his *human* friends? They *did* know what to do – because they'd been sharing *stories*. Huh had used his pictures to show his human friends what food he'd seen and where, and this helped them learn a new and incredible superpower – called *Imagination*. They used Imagination to catch that food. Then they used this superpower to think of ways they could stay alive, even though the climate was changing. And thanks to Huh and his friends using Imagination and sharing stories, humans *did* stay alive – for another **forty thousand years**.

Which means, if you think about it, that if we didn't have stories...

...*none of us* would be alive today.

Stories are *the most important thing* humans have ever invented, because they've kept us alive for...?

Forty thousand years!

Not clothes – because Nuh had those, and they didn't help.

Not tools – because Nuh had those, and they didn't help.

Not even *fire* – because Nuh had that, and it didn't help.

Stories kept human beings alive for**…? forty thousand years** – and that's why *you* are here, **forty thousand years** later!

Isn't that *amazing?!*

But that's not all. All of this means that, when your grown-ups share stories with you, your grown-ups are *the most important people in the world* – because they're doing something that has kept humans alive, for**…? Forty thousand years**.

And not only that, when *you* share stories with someone, *you* are one of the most important people in the world, because *you* are doing something that has kept humans alive – for**…? Forty thousand years!**

And who knows? If *you* share stories, maybe you'll keep humans alive for *another***…? forty thousand years!**

So now that you know how amazing and important stories are…

…would you like to hear a story?

Lesson A1:
The Most Important Invention *Ever!* (I)

Learning Objective *What will your learners 'learn', not 'do'?*	**Success Criteria** *What must the learners do to be successful?*
• Why we should be excited about hearing as many stories as possible!	• Enjoy hearing stories. • Explore books.

Resources

- A variety of age-appropriate picture books and/or *short* story books that your learners are already familiar with. To make the lesson work effectively, there should be at least 1 book per pair.

- For ages 7+, short story anthologies can be included. Chip & Korky's *Fables & Fairy Tales* series (also published by Epic Tales) is especially good for this age range.

Preparation

- Read the story of 'Huh' in advance so you are aware of the content. Consider how you may use VOICE with your learners.

- Put your resource books on display around the classroom.

Starter – *"Do Now!"*
Hooks into learning

Ask your learners:

> "What is your favourite book and why? This can be a book you have read, or one that has been read to you."

Main Input

1. Read 'Huh' to all your learners together.

2. Explain to the children that you are going to read one book to them, and they get to choose which one it is.

3. They have 5–10 minutes to look through the books and cast their vote. Votes can be names on slips of paper, cubes on books, etc.

4. Reveal the "winner", then read this book to the class.

Independent Activity
NB: This section can be skipped.

Instruct your learners:

"Recommend a book to a friend and tell them why they should read it. It can be a book you have read, seen, or had read to you."

Plenary
Choose one or more of the following...

- If you've got time, read another book together – perhaps the second place one, or have another vote!

- Talk To Your Partner:

    "How would Huh have shared these stories?"

- Give a quick hint about Lesson A2.

Check In

Talk To Your Partner:

"What have you learnt today?"

Encourage your learners to share their thoughts, but remember: *there's no need to give away the Learning Objective in these lessons.*

Lesson A1:
Behind the Scenes

'Huh' is usually the first story Chip shares when he arrives at a school, because it always serves to enthuse learners about the day ahead. It's carefully constructed to do so, of course, with several elements that leave your learners feeling empowered.

Chief among these is the reward system in the first half of the text, which releases some key chemicals into your learners' bloodstream. The questions are deliberately easy, the answer's always the same, and speaking to everyone together encourages them all to give the same answer – all of which prompts the release of three significant hormones.

One is oxytocin, the 'social hormone', a chemical that helps us feel like we're on the same side as everyone else in the room. This is an important way of putting your learners at ease.

The second is dopamine, the 'learning hormone'. This chemical heightens our senses, and makes us pay attention. We shouldn't need to tell you how *that* can be useful in the classroom! High dopamine levels are sometimes linked to anxiety – but you can be sure that won't be the case here, partly because the oxytocin will offset it.

Lastly, you'll release endorphins, the 'pleasure hormones'. Don't be concerned if your learners cheer with increasing volume every time they get an answer right – that's what you want! Combined with the subject matter, your learners will begin associating all these feelings – of ease, curiosity, and joy – with stories. And that'll be compounded when you finish Huh's tale by letting them choose a favourite story to hear.

Do not skip that part! Rather than reading their favourite story, you may be tempted to move straight to the Independent Activity, particularly with older learners. But if you do, you'll miss another major element that will help your learners fall in love with reading: the element of *choice*.

It's this moment in the lesson when your learners will feel most empowered – and rewarded; you're letting them take ownership of their experience by *investing* in it. This will encourage them to care about it, and eagerly await the 'return' they get on their investment.

So whatever happens, make sure you read the book that wins the vote. If you're worried about your learners sitting still for too long, encourage them to move during the choosing and voting process, e.g. by laying out the choices around the room.

After reading their chosen story, you then have a chance to consolidate a lot of this in the Independent Activity, especially if you also let your learners choose who they work with. They get more control this way, and more of the sheer *fun* of books (without any pressure to read), so they'll be continuing to build up their positive associations with texts.

(It's good to note that some learners will choose to work on their own – and that's fine too.

Don't worry too much if you don't have time for the Independent Activity, though. It's not essential, as the following lesson also has a strong emphasis on giving control to your learners...

Lesson A2:
Building a Story Cave

Learning Objective	**Success Criteria**
What will your learners 'learn', not 'do'?	*What must the learners do to be successful?*
• The benefits of a shared reading space.	• Understand what a comfortable space for Huh would look like. • Design a safe space. • Create a safe space as a class.

Resources

- Paper and pencils for "Do Now!"
- Paper to create the cave 'walls'.
- Paint to create hand art.
- A selection of other art/craft resources (if possible, these could be gathered during the lesson in response to the plans made by your learners).
- A selection of images of Stone Age cave dwellings.

Preparation

- Put your selection of images of Stone Age cave dwellings on display around the classroom.

Starter – "Do Now!"
Hooks into learning

Instruct your learners:

> "Draw a cave that you think Huh would find comfortable."

Stretch/Challenge:

> "Label your drawing and justify your choices."

Prior Knowledge Check

Talk To Your Partner:

> "How did Huh tell stories?"

Encourage your learners to share what they remember.

Main Input

1. Create an 'art gallery' of your learners' designs for Huh from the beginning of the lesson.
2. Send learners to walk round and view the gallery. Ask them to select one thing they like about another child's design.
3. Share feedback when back together on the carpet.

If the learners do not talk about the fact that Huh lived in the Stone Age, explore this with them. What features would a Stone Age Cave have? If they have no prior knowledge of this, draw their attention to your selection of Stone Age images to inspire them.

Independent Activity

Let your learners use the materials provided to create a cave for Huh. Carousel of activities could be…

- 'stone walls' (brick rubbings)
- 'fire' (collect sticks and add red/orange cloth to it)
- papier-mâché rocks

Once your 'stone walls' are ready, discuss with your learners what might be seen in cave paintings, then hand paint the stone walls together (as Huh would have done). Encourage the children to get inspiration from: their favourite people/pets; characters from existing stories; stories of their own.

Plenary

Attach your 'stone walls' to the walls on your teaching space, then read a book to your learners in this space.

There's more…

Check In

Talk To Your Partner:

> "What have you learnt today?"

Encourage your learners to share their thoughts, but remember: *there's no need to give away the Learning Objective in these lessons.*

Notes and Top Tips

- Beanbags make great story chairs.

- To listen to a story, your learners shouldn't sit in a circle around the 'fire' – they should sit in a clump, all facing the story 'chair', with the fire between them and the storyteller.

- The decorations need to find a space on at least three quarters of the room's walls, if not all of them.

- *Usually* the decorations are best designed to be permanent fixtures around the teaching space, but they don't need to be (see the 'Behind the Scenes' for rationales behind each option). If they must be temporary, it should be possible to put them up again quickly whenever called for, e.g. using tack, bulldog clips, etc.

Lesson A2:
Behind the Scenes

By letting your learners put their mark across your entire teaching space, you encourage them to *invest* in it – so they'll care about it, and potentially see *everything* that happens therein as a return on their investment.

Moreover, you will surround them with reminders of the empowerment they felt during Lesson A1. That alone will help them to focus whenever you (or they) bring out a book.

Finally, the Stone Age feel serves as a regular reminder of Huh's story, and of the importance of stories – so that excitement will be rekindled every time it's reading time.

Benefits of a Permanent Story Cave

In the plan, we advised that the *usual* ideal is to have this 'Story Cave' on permanent display in your classroom. This is to normalise the idea of reading. If you have to create the Cave before every reading session, *some* learners might start feeling they *need* the Cave in order to enjoy a book. You want your learners associating the joy of story with the act of *reading*, not with putting up a specific décor. A permanent Story Cave is also easier to add to (see below).

But it doesn't *have* to be permanent. Perhaps your teaching space isn't big enough, or you share it with others (e.g. you're a home tutor). Plus, the temporary method has a benefit too...

Benefit of a *Temporary* Story Cave

If your learners truly need help focusing in readiness for reading, encouraging them to reconstruct their Story Cave before a reading session (and all other lessons in this book) is a great way to provide it. This regular reminder of their investment in the reading process may especially benefit learners with ADHD.

Best of Both Worlds?

There is one way you can use your Story Cave as a tool for assisting focus without generating a reliance on it: prior to reading any book, ask your learners the question, **"Is this a book for reading *in* our story cave, or a book for reading *without* our story cave?"**

By asking this question, you open your learners to the idea that the Story Cave isn't needed every time. Moreover, you place yet more control in their hands, thus gaining even more of their investment. If they choose to read *without* the Story Cave, that's still *their* choice – they're still taking ownership of the experience.

Adding to the Story Cave

We still recommend a permanent Cave if possible, because of this one final benefit: after every story – be it one you read, one they read, or one they *make* – your learners can record it on the 'cave wall', making the space even more *theirs*.

We deliberately didn't include this in the plan, though, because we suggest you *encourage your learners to do this in their own time*, e.g. at break time. This way, you'll help them associate books with the joy and spontaneity they find in play, whilst also bringing their positive associations of break time into their teaching environment.

Through the Forest

Based on various folk tales
Written by Amy Scott Robinson
Illustrated by Korky Paul

<u>Through the forest, where leafy trees</u>
<u>Rattle and rustle with every breeze…</u>

And shadows creep on the forest floor…
A king is hunting a great white boar!
He gallops to follow his faithful hound,
But what has that barking and baying dog found?

Not the white boar that the king was stalking,
But a boy and girl who are carefully walking…

<u>Through the forest, where leafy trees</u>
<u>Rattle and rustle with every breeze…</u>

The boy drops crumbs along the track
To leave a trail to lead them back –
Although his clever plan will fail,
For hungry birds are eating the trail,
And as the kids begin to cry,
They turn a corner and suddenly spy…?

<u>Through the forest, where leafy trees</u>
<u>Rattle and rustle with every breeze…</u>

A girl, who's wearing a scarlet hood
And gathering flowers around the wood.
But in the shadows, unseen by the child,
A wolf – who is scary and hairy and wild –
Is licking his lips and loping ahead
To a quaint little house where he hides in bed.
But...?

Through the forest, where leafy trees,
Rattle and rustle with every breeze...

A daddy and mummy and baby bear
Are on their way home; who's hiding there?
A princess! *She* hid from her stepmother queen,
And there in the cottage she started to clean
Seven small chairs and seven small beds –
Until, with an apple all rosy and red...

Through the forest, where leafy trees,
Rattle and rustle with every breeze...

An old man searched for the perfect rose
To give his daughter the gift she chose.
Unknown to him, the rose he stole
Belongs to—
      A dragon?
             No – a beast!
                    No, a troll!

<u>Through the forest, where leafy trees,</u>
<u>Rattle and rustle with every breeze...</u>

A beauty is rushing to rescue her dad,
A prince asks seven small men why they're sad,
Three bears find Goldilocks sleeping in bed,
A woodcutter races to save Little Red,
A witch adds a sweet to her gingerbread door,
And a king is still hunting a great white boar...

Forests are places with magic inside,
Where mystical creatures and fairy tales hide.
If you don't believe me, just come and see –
Find a forest, and walk with me...

Through the forest, where leafy trees,
Rattle and rustle with every breeze...

Lesson A3:
Fun on the Page

Learning Objective
What will your learners 'learn', not 'do'?

- To explore, and delight in, the sound of words, then link that delight to reading.

Success Criteria
What must the learners do to be successful?

- Explore new words.
- Choose words that they take delight in.
- Explore the sounds words make.

Resources

- Paper and drawing/colouring materials.
- Magpie sheet for children's sketches/ideas/magpied words.

Preparation

- Read the story of '**Through the Forest**' in advance so you are aware of the content. Consider how you may use VOICE with your learners.

Starter – *"Do Now!"*
Hooks into learning

Give groups of learners a list of 9 words that they can read (these need to be matched with the level your learners are working at) and ask them to rank these words with their favourite word first. They need to be able to explain why they have put them in that order, and why the top word is their favourite.

Prior Knowledge Check

Talk To Your Partner:

"What are some of your favourite words, and what do they mean?"

Encourage your learners to share their thoughts.

Main Input

1. Read **'Through the Forest'** to all your learners together.

2. Talk To Your Partner:

    "What did you like about the poem and why?"

    Record the children's ideas for your reading wall.

3. Talk To Your Partner:

    "What *language/words/vocabulary* in the poem do you like?"

    Lead with a few of your favourite examples (moments of rhyme, alliteration, 'fun-sounding' words, moments of surprise).

NB: You and your learners may find it useful to re-read the poem verse by verse.

Independent Activity

Instruct your learners to record their favourite words and/or phrases on a magpie sheet. They may include illustrations as well.

Scaffold: Print out the poem so that learners can highlight and copy the parts they want to magpie.

Challenge/Stretch: Ask your learners to define the words they have selected, either by using a dictionary or inferring from the context of the words in the sentence.

Plenary

Share the words/phrases the children have selected to magpie and add some of them to your reading wall.

Check In

Talk To Your Partner:

"What have you learnt today?"

Encourage your learners to share their thoughts, but remember: *there's no need to give away the Learning Objective in these lessons.*

Magpie Sheet

Lesson A3:
Behind the Scenes

Our brains are naturally attracted to patterns. We can't get enough of 'em! This mental magnetism to methodology can be linked to all sorts of human endeavours, from maths to murder mysteries, drumming to dancing, textiles to spotting deities in burnt toast. And pattern play is abundant in childhood games, from the card-matching of Snap to the button combinations of console "beat-'em-ups".

Pattern passion undoubtedly had a role to play in the development of language, too, as was first spotted (or at least, first recorded) by the philosophers Socrates, Plato, and Aristotle. This trio noticed that the *sound* of words could be so beautiful that they would emotively captivate an audience – even to the point where they begin to believe the speaker/writer's story regardless of any facts (or lack thereof). Such is the art of rhetoric.

But though rhetoric has got something of a bad press in its recent years of political abuse, it continues to be a mainstay of children's fiction. The rhetorical tool of alliteration, for instance, can be seen in the titles of such literary greats as Julia Donaldson (*A Squash and a Squeeze*), Roald Dahl (*James and the Giant Peach*), and Michael Morpurgo (*Kensuke's Kingdom*).

So by taking the time to focus on the language of a text in this way, you'll take advantage of your learners' natural propensity for the pleasure of patterns, helping them to associate that enjoyment with reading. By recognising and celebrating the playfulness that pitter-patters across the pages of their favourite stories, they'll begin to appreciate how this language actually helps tp *make* those stories their favourites.

And at the same time, by delighting in these less common words and phrases, you'll be assisting them in the assimilation of a richer vocab.

In the world of primary (and secondary) education, the tools of rhetoric are most often considered when discussing poetry – especially those tools like alliteration, rhythm, and rhyme. Indeed, that's one of the reasons we've used a poem for this lesson. But the greatest works of prose also abound in plucky punctuation, bouncing beats, and lyrical tickles – as you'll doubtless discover when you begin using this "Recyclable Lesson" with other texts too. Your learners certainly shall.

Lesson A4:
Story Links (I)

Learning Objective
What will your learners 'learn', not 'do'?

- A basic understanding of how books are connected.

Success Criteria
What must the learners do to be successful?

- Find books that link to the **'Through the Forest'** Poem.
- (Optional) Understand and use the Opening technique in storytelling.
- (Optional) Write an extra verse for the poem based on the books they find.

Resources

- Worksheet/reading journal for your learners to record the books they find.

Either…

- gather an assortment of children's books, many of which (but not all) should contain references to forests

or…

- arrange to deliver this lesson in a library – school library, local library, or bus.

Preparation

- Make sure you are familiar and confident in the use of the Opening technique mentioned in **Chapter 6** of this book.
- Find two contrasting examples for you to model during the Main Input.

Starter – *"Do Now!"*
Hooks into learning

Instruct your learners:

"Write, draw, or talk about as many stories as you can that are forest-based. Remember that there were lots of stories in the poem we heard. Be ready to share your ideas!"

Prior Knowledge Check

Talk To Your Partner:

"What were your favourite words from the 'Through the Forest' Poem? Be ready to share your partner's choice."

Encourage your learners to share what they remember.

Main Input

Put your learners in teams, then **challenge** them to find and record as many books as possible that could have been used in the 'Through the Forest' poem. The books they record *must* contain the words "trees", "wood", or "forest" (this is important so that your learners understand the links to the poem).

Advise your learners that pictures can give us clues to the words that might be on the page – but *only clues*. **Model** two contrasting examples, such as...

1. In *The Gruffalo* there is a picture of a mouse in a wood, and the first line reads, "A mouse took a stroll through the deep dark wood".

2. In *The Gingerbread Man*, there is a picture of a forest, but the words "forest," "wood," and even "trees" don't appear on any of the pages.

Ask your learners:

"Can I record either of these books in this challenge? Why/why not?"

Encourage your learners to talk and then share their thoughts. Ensure they understand that they can use Example 1 because they have found the *word* "wood", but they can't use Example 2 as it doesn't contain the *words* "forest", "wood", or "trees".

Let your learners know that there will be a prize if *every* team gets a score of at least 2 (for ages 4–5), 4 (for ages 5–7), or 6 (for ages 7+). **NB: You know your learners best, so ensure that the goal is achievable for all of them.**

There's more...

Lesson A4: Story Links (I)   All the Better to Read You With   75

Independent Activity

Your learners search the selection of books available in their teams.

After *at least* 10 minutes, end the challenge.

Each team calculates their points, scoring one point for each book that definitely includes one of the words. *Every team needs to hit the target.* If a group is struggling, encourage learners who have already found the words to support those who haven't.

Plenary

1. Encourage your learners to get excited about their prize: you're going to read their choice of a forest story to them right now!

2. Your learners vote on the forest-based story to have read to them.

3. Read their chosen story aloud and use the Opening technique before any instance of the word "forest", "trees", or "wood", encouraging your learners to join in with that word and then cheer.

Optional Extra 1

Split your learners into small groups to read one of the forest-themed books to each other, encouraging them to use the Opening technique modelled in the Plenary.

Optional Extra 2

Let your learners work in small groups, pairs, and/or as individuals to write a new verse for the '**Through the Forest**' poem based on at least one of the books they have found.

Check In

Talk To Your Partner:

"What have you learnt today?"

Encourage your learners to share their thoughts, but remember: *there's no need to give away the Learning Objective in these lessons.*

Reading Journal
Books that could have been used in 'Through the Forest'

Lesson A4:
Behind the Scenes

Here (and with the second 'Story Links' lesson later in this Volume) you're encouraging your learners to find links between a story they've enjoyed, words on *other* pages they've enjoyed, and words on pages they're maybe *yet* to enjoy – all the while giving them a fun challenge that stimulates their curiosity, their delight in colourful artwork, and a little of their competitive spirit.

As well as nurturing an association of pleasure with books, this lesson nurtures an association of *books* with books. The sooner your learners realise that one story can lead to another, the sooner they'll develop an appetite for independent reading.

While this is meant to be a challenge, it's important to set a target that you're confident all your learners will hit. This will allow you to follow the activity with the reward of another read, thereby further cementing your learners' association of reading with feelings such as achievement, satisfaction, and success.

One Lost Slipper

Based on the accounts of Herodotus, Strabo, and Aelian
Adapted & written by Chip Colquhoun
Illustrated by Mario Coelho

I have a secret for you – one of the biggest secrets in the *world*. Almost nobody knows this secret, and I bet it will surprise all the grown-ups you know.

But before I can share this secret with you, I need to tell you a story – and it's really quite a sad story. The girl in this story is treated really horribly by the other girls in her house, and they even stop her going to a party for none other than *the prince*.

Don't get too upset, though – the girl gets a happy ending, I promise. In fact, she even ends up *marrying* the prince. Oh, and this story also involves a very special pair of slippers...

...and the name of the girl in this story is...?

Rhodopis.

You see, about 2,600 years ago, at the start of this story, Rhodopis was happy. She lived on the island of Samos, which is near the warm country of Greece, and she began every day by going to the sandy beach. There she would dance, and sing, and laugh delightedly.

Her friends from the sea loved to come and watch Rhodopis dance. These friends were turtles, dolphins, and starfish, and they all sang to her the words,

Rosy-cheeked Rhodopis,
Everybody's hope is
Your dance and song and laughter
Make you happy ever after.

Except it didn't sound *exactly* like that. The turtles sang with a low, booming voice, like this...

ROHsy-CHEEKked RhoDOHpis,
EHverybody's HOHpe is,
Your DAHnce and SOHng and LAHghter
Make you HAHppy EHver AHfter.

I'll sing like a turtle again, and you can join in if you like...

ROHsy-CHEEKked RhoDOHpis,
EHverybody's HOHpe is,
Your DAHnce and SOHng and LAHghter
Make you HAHppy EHver AHfter.

The dolphins, though, sang with a bouncy voice, like this...

Roh-oh-oh-sy-chee-ee-ee-ked Rhodoh-oh-oh-oh-pis,
Eh-eh-vryboh-oh-oh-dy's hoh-oh-oh-ope is
Your dah-ah-ah-ahnce and soh-oh-oh-ong and lah-ah-ah-ghter
Make you hah-ah-ah-appy eh-eh-eh-ever ah-ah-ah-after.

I'll sing like a dolphin again, you can join in with *them* if you like...

Roh-oh-oh-sy-chee-ee-ee-ked Rhodoh-oh-oh-oh-pis,
Eh-eh-vryboh-oh-oh-dy's hoh-oh-oh-ope is
Your dah-ah-ah-ahnce and soh-oh-oh-ong and lah-ah-ah-ghter
Make you hah-ah-ah-appy eh-eh-eh-ever ah-ah-ah-after.

The starfish, however, sang with a high, cute voice, like this...

Reeoosy-cheeeeked Reeoodeeoopis,
Eeevree-bawdee's heeoope is
Your deeance and seeong and leeaughter
Meek you heeappy eeever eearfter.

I'll sing like a starfish again, you can join in with them as well, if you like…

Reeoosy-cheeeeked Reeoodeeoopis,
Eeevree-bawdee's heeoope is
Your deeance and seeong and leeaughter
Meek you heeappy eeever eearfter.

But of course they all sang together – so how about you sing the song as your favourite, turtle or dolphin or starfish, and we'll hear exactly what Rhodopis would have heard…

ROHsy-CHEEKked RhoDOHpis,
Eh-eh-vryboh-oh-oh-dy's hoh-oh-oh-ope is
Your dah-ah-ah-ahnce and soh-oh-oh-ong and lah-ah-ah-ghter
Meek you heeappy eeever eearfter.

Rhodopis thought their singing was beautiful! It made her happy at the start of every single day.

But then came the day when she arrived at the beach and saw a huge sailing ship. Some large, strong, serious sailors came out from that ship, and they chased Rhodopis along the sandy shore. At last they caught her, and they dragged her, kicking and screaming, all the way back to the ship.

Rhodopis was thrown into a dark, damp room at the bottom of the ship, where there were many other men and women who had been stolen from their homes. The ship left the Greek island and set off across the sea, and soon a huge storm began to blow, causing huge waves to rock the ship violently from side to side. The other prisoners were terrified!

Rhodopis didn't feel too scared, though – because she could hear the turtles swimming beneath the ship, the dolphins swimming alongside the ship, and the starfish clinging to the side of the ship, each of them singing... Well, do you remember what they were singing?

<u>ROHsy-CHEEKked RhoDOHpis,</u>
<u>Eh-eh-vryboh-oh-oh-dy's hoh-oh-oh-ope is</u>
<u>Your dah-ah-ah-ahnce and soh-oh-oh-ong and lah-ah-ah-ghter</u>
<u>Meek you heeappy eeever eearfter.</u>

After the ship had sailed through the storm, it travelled down a long river called the Nile into a country called Egypt, and eventually came to a large city called Memphis. There, the strong men took the prisoners to the market, so the rich people of Egypt could buy them to work as slaves in their houses.

One of these rich Egyptians was a very old man called Xanthes. When Xanthes saw Rhodopis, he thought she would make a beautiful slave. So he bought her, and he gave her the easiest job of all his slaves: waving a large leaf fan to keep Xanthes cool during the hot Egyptian days. Rhodopis had such a simple job that it made all the *other* slaves rather jealous.

But Xanthes was *very* old, and any grown-up will tell you that the older you get, the more naps you need to take. And as soon as Xanthes went for a nap, the other slaves all went over to Rhodopis and said things like,

"Rhodopis? Sweep the floor for me. I'm off to have a little nap."

"Rhodopis? Clean the toilets for me. I'm off to play a little game."

"Rhodopis? Wash the clothes for me. I'm off to have a little walk. No, *you* can't come – *you're too busy!*"

Off went the slaves, leaving Rhodopis to do all those tough jobs by herself. How do you think that made Rhodopis feel?

But while *most* slaves may have felt upset and bullied, Rhodopis actually didn't mind too much – because in those days, that last job? Washing the clothes? That had to be done in the clean water of the River Nile. And after washing the clothes and hanging them from the branches of a tree to dry, Rhodopis had the bank of the river all to herself – where she danced and sang and laughed just like she'd done back at her home on Samos island.

True, the turtles and dolphins and starfish couldn't come down the Nile to join her. But there *were* hippos, and crocodiles, and ibis birds – and all of these became new friends for Rhodopis, enjoying her dancing and singing and laughing, and singing her song…

So now: if you're going to join in with the song *this* time, you'll need to use the voice of a hippo, a crocodile, or an ibis bird (which is like an Egyptian pelican, a bird with a very long beak). How would the song sound if sung by a hippo, a crocodile, or a bird with a very long beak? If you like, pick one to try, then join in with me…

<u>Rosy-cheeked Rhodopis,</u>
<u>Everybody's hope is</u>
<u>Your dance and song and laughter</u>
<u>Make you happy ever after.</u>

One day, Xanthes happened to be out for a walk when he heard Rhodopis singing down by the river. He followed the sound of her wonderful voice until he saw her magnificent dancing – her whirls, her twirls, and the swirling curls of her hair. Xanthes was so delightedly dazzled by her dancing that he cried, "Feet like those should have dancing shoes!"

Xanthes took Rhodopis to a shoemaker in the city, and asked them to make a pair of dancing shoes that would fit Rhodopis' feet perfectly. He told the shoemaker to make them with rose gold, so they would look as stunning as Rhodopis herself.

And so the shoemaker crafted a pair of beautiful rose-gold slippers. When the slippers were given to Rhodopis, she pulled them onto her feet – and instantly fell in love with them! They sparkled and shone, making her dancing even more bedazzling and beguiling! Rhodopis felt the happiest she'd been in a long time.

And all the *other* slaves felt the most *jealous* they'd been in a long time. They couldn't wait for a chance to get some revenge on Rhodopis.

And, sure enough, their chance came.

You see, the Prince of Egypt was a young man called Psamtik, and he had decided to have a huge party for everyone in Memphis. *Everyone* in Memphis – slaves included.

When Prince Psamtik's party invitation arrived at Xanthes' house, Xanthes was *so excited* that... he needed to take a nap. After all, he *was* extremely elderly.

As soon as he disappeared into his bedroom, though, all the envious slaves went to Rhodopis and said things like,

"*Rhodopis?* Sweep the floor for me. I'm off to the prince's party."

"*Rhodopis?* Clean the toilets for me. I'm off to the prince's party."

"*Rhodopis?* Wash the clothes for me. I'm off to the prince's party. No, *you* can't come – *you're too busy!*"

Off went the other slaves, leaving Rhodopis to do all those dispiriting jobs solitarily. How do you think that made Rhodopis feel *now*?

Well *now*, she *did* feel upset and bullied – and really rather cross! She was looking forward to dancing at a royal party with her fabulous rose-gold slippers – it would be so wondrous! She desperately rushed to finish all those extra jobs as fast as she could, snatching the washing basket and stomping down to the river where–

Oh! She slipped – and fell sideways into a patch of wet, sticky mud! The filth clung to her slippers – yes, her gorgeous rose-gold slippers!

Now Rhodopis was even *more* furious. She hastily washed her slippers in the Nile first, then left them on the riverbank, hoping they would dry by the time she had finished hanging out the rest of the washing.

What Rhodopis didn't know was that, from the top of a tree, she was being watched. There on the highest branch sat a feathery falcon, a bird with a small beak but longer wings than a hawk. But this wasn't an ordinary falcon. This was an Egyptian god in disguise – the Egyptian god Horus.

Horus was the Egyptian god with the job of caring for the royal family. But right now, as he looked down at Rhodopis, he said to himself…

<u>Rosy-cheeked Rhodopis,</u>
<u>Everybody's hope is</u>
<u>Your dance and song and laughter</u>
<u>Make you happy ever after…</u>

Suddenly, the falcon swooped down, snatched up one of Rhodopis' rose-gold slippers, and flew swiftly into the distance – leaving Rhodopis gasping, yelling, and desperately pleading for the falcon to bring it back. But as the bird disappeared from view, Rhodopis collapsed to her knees, dropped her head into her hands, and cried and cried and cried…

Meanwhile, Prince Psamtik was sitting on his throne in the Great Hall of Memphis, watching everyone arriving for his party. He was especially watching the women, because he was looking to find…? a *wife*.

That was the whole reason why the prince had put on the party! He wanted to find a wife. And he wasn't worried about whether his wife was rich or poor. He was the prince! He was rich enough already. He just wanted a wife who would be caring and kind, but clever and brave – and if she was a good dancer as well, that would be a bonus!

Just then, a falcon swooped into the hall through the large open doors, catching the prince's eye. Psamtik watched the falcon fly right above his head. Then the falcon dropped something.

Psamtik caught it: a single rose-gold slipper.

Psamtik watched the falcon fly off through one of the hall's tall open windows, then looked down at the slipper. It was delicate and dainty, but bright and bold – and suddenly, Psamtik realised what was going on!

He stood up and declared, "This is a sign from Horus! The woman whose foot fits this shoe perfectly must be the woman I am destined to marry!"

So what do you think Prince Psamtik did next?

He didn't go around trying the slipper on all the women in Memphis *himself* – he was a prince, so he had servants to do it for him. Those servants took the slipper to every house in Memphis, but couldn't find a single woman whose foot fit within it.

And when they brought the slipper to the house of Xanthes…

…they *still* didn't find a single woman whose foot fit in the slipper. Not even any of the slaves.

But as the prince's men were leaving Xanthes' house, they heard singing from down by the Nile. They followed the sound until they found Rhodopis dancing along the riverbank.

When Rhodopis tried the slipper on, it fit her positively perfectly – and the servants were even more convinced when Rhodopis showed them the other slipper.

And so Rhodopis married Prince Psamtik, and the girl who had once been a Greek slave became a caring, kind, clever, and brave Egyptian princess – who was also *exceptionally* excellent at dancing.

Rhodopis and Psamtik had a

wedding at the point where the Nile meets the sea, so that *all* Rhodopis' friends could be there: the hippos, the crocodiles, and the ibis birds, but also the turtles, the dolphins, and the starfish, all of them singing…

You know what they were singing, don't you? If you want to, pick the sound of your favourite animal friend, and join in…

Rosy-cheeked Rhodopis,
Everybody's hope is
Your dance and song and
    laughter
Make you happy ever after.

The End

Psst! Reading this out loud to your learners for the first time? You're not actually finished yet – turn the page…

And now you know that story, I can share with you this humungous secret. I just want to ask you, though: when I said at the start that the girl in this story is treated really horribly by other girls in her house, but it all ends happily because she ends up marrying the prince, and I mentioned that there'd be a very special pair of slippers…

…who did you *think* this story was going to be about?

Many people have heard how *Cinderella* was treated horrendously by her stepmother and stepsisters, but her fairy godmother gave her some glass slippers to wear at the prince's ball. Did you spot anything in the story of Rhodopis that sounded like the story of Cinderella?

But about 2,500 years before today, a historian called Herodotus wrote a history book saying that, about *2,600* years before today, there lived a Greek girl called Rhodopis on the island of Samos, who ended up as a slave to a man in Memphis called Xanthes…

…a historian called Strabo wrote a history book telling how a falcon stole one of Rhodopis' shoes…

…and a historian called Aelian wrote a history book recounting how that slipper was dropped in the lap of an Egyptian prince called Psamtik.

The story of Rhodopis was told all around Egypt and Greece, and some travellers took it to Ancient Rome. The Romans liked the story too, and told it wherever they went. The Romans went to a *lot* of places, like the land we now called Germany. And somewhere in that land, a mother wanted to tell the story to her children – but suddenly thought,

"Oo, hold on. We don't have slaves here, so my children won't know what that means. I know! I'll call them horrid stepsisters. Ah, but my children don't know anything about Egyptian gods like Horus… I know! I'll say it was a fairy godmother instead! Oo! And my children have never seen rose gold, but they know that *glass* is a precious material for making slippers!

"There's just one more thing. 'Rhodopis' sounds like a strange name to us, because we're not Greek. I know! This girl is going to be given all sorts of tough jobs to do, like cleaning the chimney, so she'll get completely covered in the ash and *cinders* from the fire…

"So I know! I'll call her…

Aschenputtel!"

And that mother told the story of Aschenputtel to her children, and her children told that story to their friends, and their friends told it to *their* friends, who told it to *their* friends who told it to *their* friends...

...and eventually the story ended up in France, where someone said, "Aschenputtel? I think it'll sound nicer if we call her *Cinderella*."

Which means, if you think about it...

...Cinderella is based on a *true story!* Her real name was Rhodopis, who was a *real person* living around 2,600 years ago!

What will your grown-ups say when you tell them *that?!*

Lesson A5:
Where Stories Come From (I)

Learning Objective	**Success Criteria**
What will your learners 'learn', not 'do'?	*What must the learners do to be successful?*
• How books help us discover more about our history and the world.	• Decide which parts of stories might be true, and which might be imagined.

Resources

- A table (either on a board or flipchart) with 2 columns – one headed "TRUE?", the other headed "IMAGINED?"
- A worksheet version of this table for your learners.

Preparation

- Read the story of **'One Lost Slipper'** in advance so you are aware of the content. Consider how you may use VOICE with your learners.

Starter – *"Do Now!"*
Hooks into learning

Instruct your learners:

> "Retell the story of Cinderella in a pair/group."

Prior Knowledge Check

Talk To Your Partner:

> "What does the word 'true' mean?
> What does the word 'imagined' mean?"

Encourage your learners to share their thoughts.

Main Input

1. Read **'One Lost Slipper'** to your learners. Ensure you take the time to enjoy the discussion around the similarities between Rhodopis and Cinderella.

2. Point out that, even though this story is in history books, there is still a 100-year gap between Herodotus and Rhodopis.

3. Talk To Your Partner and be ready to feedback...

    "Do you think Herodotus ever met Rhodopis?"

    "If they did meet, would Rhodopis or Herodotus remember everything in the story perfectly?"

4. Show your learners the table. Highlight that "True?" and "Imagined?" both have question marks because we can't be sure – so we're only writing what we think.

5. **Model** putting 'Rhodopis liked to dance by the beach' in the "True?" column and encourage your learners to discuss your choice.

6. Continue to complete the table for **'One Lost Slipper'** as a class. If they think someone made up that the sea creatures came to watch her dance, for example, you would put that in the "Imagined?" column.
    Explain to the children that there are no wrong answers, but it is okay to challenge what each other think – debate is good.

Independent Activity

Using a fairy tale of their choice that they know well, instruct your learners to complete another table either as pairs, groups, or on their own.

NB: You can provide books for your learners to use for this activity if you feel this will be accessible for them. However, this activity works best with books of known fairy/folk tales.

Plenary

Share your learners' independent activity, perhaps using a visualiser/projector. Do any learners have anything to add to each other's tables?

Check In

Talk To Your Partner:

"What have you learnt today?"

Encourage your learners to share their thoughts, but remember: *there's no need to give away the Learning Objective in these lessons.*

True?

Imagined?

Lesson A5:
Behind the Scenes

Were *you* surprised to learn that Cinderella is based on a true story? Rhodopis is often thought of as 'the Egyptian Cinderella' (indeed, Shirley Climo wrote a wonderful picture book of that name, gorgeously and stylistically illustrated by Ruth Heller). But she is more accurately referred to as 'the *first* Cinderella'. And because she almost definitely existed, that means, yep: Cinders is based on a real woman.

The word "almost" is important there, though. We can never be 100% confident about the accuracy of ancient historical records – for multiple reasons, not least being the bias of the historians. That's why you put the question mark after the headings of *both* columns, and stress for your learners that there are no wrong answers here.

But however much of Rhodopis' tale is true, the fact it spread to several corners of the ancient world is a testament to how easily it enamoured those who heard it – which brings us, as ever, back to that *B-M-E* of story.

"Is that story real?"

This is one of the most popular questions from young learners after hearing any tale, by which they usually mean, "Was that story *true?*" They're likely asking this because of how the story is affecting them neurologically: they feel compelled to consider what they've just heard for 'life lessons', which are real-life applications, so naturally they want to know the likelihood that *they* could end up in a similar situation as the tale's hero.

The most accurate answer to a question like this is probably, "Partly…" – but for most stories, that would take some long and complex discussion.

With this lesson, though, the story of Rhodopis helps you to lay the foundation for those discussions. Yes, parts of the story *are* real – as are parts of Cinderella. But exactly *which* parts is a matter of exploration, consideration, and opinion (you can tell your learners that these combine to make our 'intuition').

And so a story, however real, helps us to discover more about the *definitely* real world around us.

After this lesson, it'll be high time to let your learners in on the most basic principle of what a story needs: the *B*.

And, after this lesson, they'll be ready to hear it…

Lesson A6: What a Story Needs

Learning Objective
What will your learners 'learn', not 'do'?

- How to identify the first essential element of a good story: the *Bad Thing*.

Success Criteria
What must the learners do to be successful?

- Identify "bad things" that happen in stories.
- Understand how these are actually important for a story.
- Unpick a story of their choice (i.e. identify how the "bad things" are important for that story).

Resources

- A table (either on a board or flipchart) with 2 columns – one headed "I don't like it when…", the other headed "…but that's good because…"
- A worksheet version of this table for your learners.

Preparation

- Find the alternative endings to **'One Lost Slipper'** (which begin on page 100) and read them in advance so you are aware of the content. In particular, note how the words "the end" should be delivered plainly and without ceremony, within the final sentence. Bookmark the pages with these endings so it's easy to flip between them and the story.

Starter – *"Do Now!"*
Hooks into learning

Instruct your learners to write/draw/discuss the answer to this question:

"What are the bad things that happen in the story of **'One Lost Slipper'**? Be ready to share what you have remembered."

Prior Knowledge Check

Share the bad things that your learners have remembered from the story, and draw their attention to any that they have not remembered.

Main Input

Explain that you're going to read the story of '**One Lost Slipper**' again, but this time you'll give your learners the chance to rescue Rhodopis before things get too bad for her.

Begin the story from the words, "...about 2,600 years ago..." – and there's no need to demonstrate the voices of the sea creatures before inviting your learners to join in.

Crisis points are marked in the text with a number of slippers corresponding to one of the alternative endings. At each crisis point, pause and ask your learners:

"Shall we rescue Rhodopis?"

If *anyone* responds "Yes," read the corresponding alternative ending.

After finishing each alternative ending, ask your learners if that version was better than before, when she ended up marrying the prince. If *anyone* says "No!", continue with the original tale. This time, stop when you reach "The End".

Talk To Your Partner:

"Do you think Rhodopis would have had her happy ending without the challenges? Why/why not?"

Lead a discussion with your learners about how Rhodopis needed to go through her challenges in order to have her happy ending.

As part of this, introduce the table and **model** completing it – for example...

1. "I don't like it when..." *"the strong men catch Rhodopis"*
   "...but that's good because..." *"it gets Rhodopis closer to her prince"*

2. "I don't like it when..." *"the slaves bully Rhodopis"*
   "...but that's good because..." *"she gets to dance by the river so Xanthes buys her the special slippers"*

Encourage your learners to give their ideas to help you complete the table.

There's more...

Independent Activity

Using a fairy tale of their choice that they know well, instruct your learners to complete another table either as pairs, groups, or on their own.

NB: You can provide books for your learners to use for this activity if you feel this will be accessible for them. However, note that this is a Recyclable lesson – so you may wish to prevent your learners using any book that you intend to read together at a later date.

Plenary

Share your learners' independent activity, perhaps using a visualiser/projector. Do any learners have anything to add to each other's tables?

Check In

Talk To Your Partner:

> "What have you learnt today?"

Encourage your learners to share their thoughts, but remember: *there's no need to give away the Learning Objective in these lessons.*

...but that's good because...

I don't like it when...

One Lost Slipper: Alternative Endings

Then came the day when Rhodopis arrived at the beach and saw a huge sailing ship. Some large, strong, serious sailors came out of it, but Rhodopis hid behind a tree so they didn't see her. The ship went away, and Rhodopis got to live fairly happily for the rest of her life, the end.

Rhodopis went and woke Xanthes up to tell him that the other slaves were being mean bullies. Xanthes got so angry with those slaves that he told them they would all have to stay at home, and Rhodopis was the only one who got to go to the prince's party. There she had a really lovely dance, but there were thousands of other women there too – so she didn't get to meet the prince. She didn't mind, though, and afterwards she went back to Xanthes' house to wave a leafy fan and live fairly happily for the rest of her life, the end.

Rhodopis went and woke Xanthes up to tell him that the other slaves were being mean bullies. Xanthes got so angry with those slaves that he sent them all away, and bought better slaves to take their place. So Rhodopis got to wave a leafy fan and live fairly happily for the rest of her life, the end.

Oh! Rhodopis slipped – but she quickly grabbed hold of a branch and stopped herself from landing in the wet, sticky mud! She felt a joyous relief that she hadn't dirtied her gorgeous rose-gold slippers, and this gave her the energy to complete the washing nice and quickly. So she *did* get to the prince's party – but by the time she got there, the prince had found a wife from among the women. She didn't mind, though, and had a really lovely dance before heading back to Xanthes' house to wave a leafy fan and live fairly happily for the rest of her life, the end.

Suddenly, Horus swooped down and said, "Rhodopis! Forget the washing! I am the god who looks after the royal family, and I think you'll be a perfect wife for Prince Psamtik! Get yourself to his party, now!" So Rhodopis dropped everything and ran to Psamtik's party. There she went up to the prince to tell him what Horus had said to her.

But Psamtik said, "You're saying a bird spoke to you? Ha! That's crazy! If Horus wanted me to marry you, he would give me a sign – but the only sign I'm getting right now is that you are mad! You'll be trying to tell me that crocodiles and hippos can sing next! Guards? Make sure this bonkers person doesn't get near me again."

So Rhodopis just went back to the dancefloor. She didn't mind, though, because she had a really lovely dance before heading back to Xanthes' house to wave a leafy fan and live fairly happily for the rest of her life, the end.

Lesson A6:
Behind the Scenes

How better to demonstrate the importance of the Bad Thing for a story than to take it away? And while the alternative endings may amuse your learners, they will help to carry home the point: Rhodopis could have enjoyed an *easier* life, but that wouldn't necessarily have been *better*.

This is one reason why you should read an alternative ending even if you only get a single learner calling for it. Likewise, you should continue with the main story even if only a minority of your learners think the alternative is not good enough. An additional benefit to this is that you reinforce the idea that *every opinion matters* – and since they all get the alternative *and* the original ending, ultimately everyone wins.

(In the event *all* of your learners want to stick with an alternative ending, let *yourself* be the one who wants to read on. There's no harm in encouraging your learners to see that *your* opinion matters too...!)

By allowing your learners to focus on the crisis points in a tale, you help to enhance their 'story sense'. The guilty pleasure of putting peril in the path of a character we're invested in... The joy of seeing that character triumph... The satisfaction of the happy ending showing that the peril was worth it... All this is building your learners' innate understanding of the pleasure of reading.

And not only will this leave them more inclined to seek that pleasure out for themselves, but it comes with two bumper bonuses. First, your learners will be more motivated to learn the art of reading independently.

Second, your learners will be more equipped to notice the signs of a good story in the early pages of *longer* texts, giving them the motivation they need to conquer chapter books.

In other words, this lesson is a major first step in helping your learners to build their 'reading stamina'. Hence why we've made this one Recyclable – make the "I don't like it / but it's good" exercise a regular follow-up to *any* fiction they read, and you'll further enshrine the fun to be found in books.

Tiger's Terror

Based on a Chinese folk tale
Adapted & written by Chip Colquhoun
Illustrated by Mario Coelho

A fox took a stroll in a wood one day
When a tiger leapt out in the fox's way.
"My favourite food!" the tiger said,
And bared all the teeth in its stripey head.
Each tooth was as sharp as the vicious claws
On the turned-out toes of its monstrous paws.
With stripes of orange and stripes of black,
The tiger prepared for a foxy snack!

However, the fox, though rather small,
Did not look the least bit scared at all.
"Your favourite food?" declared the fox,
"Well *that* is the poppiest of poppycocks!
The mightiest beast in the woods is *me* –
When *I* travel by, all other beasts flee!
You think that I'm wrong? or that I deceive?
Come strolling with me – you will soon believe!"

The words of the fox made the tiger laugh,
So much you could fill a whole paragraph
With its "Ha!" and its "Ho!" and its "Tee hee hee!"
Till at last it replied, "Oh you tickle me!
A furball like you couldn't cause a scare."
Said the fox, "But I do! I breakfast on bear.
I've a lion for lunch, then a man for tea."
Said the curious tiger, "Alright, let's see."

They walked and they walked till the small fox said,
"Oh look! There's a bear on the path ahead!"
The bear heard the fox, but saw *tiger* there,
For the tiger was the biggest of the furry pair.
Said the bear, "Oh, I'm late to catch Goldilocks!
I must run – as must *you* run as *well*, friend fox!"
"Soon," said the fox as the big bear fled.
"Amazing!" the now-nervous tiger said.

They walked and they walked till the small fox said,
"Oh look! There's a lion on the path ahead!"
The lion heard the fox, but saw *tiger* there,
For the tiger was the biggest of the furry pair.
Said the lion, "Is it lunchtime? I forgot my clocks!
I must run – as must *you* run as *well*, friend fox!"
"Soon," said the fox as the large lion fled.
"Astounding!" the *more*-nervous tiger said.

They walked and they walked till the small fox said,
"Oh look! There's a man on the path ahead!"
The man heard the fox, but saw tiger there,
For the tiger was the biggest of the furry pair.
Said the man, "You know what? I forgot my socks!
I must run – as must *you* run as *well*, friend fox!"
"Soon," said the fox as the man made haste,
"But I now want to learn just how *tigers* taste…"

"How *tigers* taste?!" the tiger said,
And the fox said, "Time for some *tiger bread!*"
At that, the tiger was filled with fear,
And declared, "Now *I'm* getting out of here!"
It fled just as fast as the fastest wind,
But the fox didn't chase – it just sat and grinned.
For the fox knew that tiger's entire error
Was to miss how the fox borrowed tiger's terror.

Lesson A7:
Where Stories Come From (II)

Learning Objective
What will your learners 'learn', not 'do'?
• How some of our favourite picture books are inspired by older stories.

Success Criteria
What must the learners do to be successful?
• Make connections between stories.
• Use the pattern of a story they know to create their own.
• Share their story either by retelling, drawing, and/or writing.

Resources

- A copy of *The Gruffalo* (optional).
- Paper and drawing media.
- Images of small and large animals (modern, prehistoric, and/or fictitious).
- Copies of the story for the Independent Activity.

Preparation

- Read the story of **'Tiger's Terror'** in advance so you are aware of the content. Consider how you may use VOICE with your learners.
- If you plan to present a copy of *The Gruffalo* for your learners, keep it somewhere hidden but easily accessible.

Starter – *"Do Now!"*
Hooks into learning

Instruct your learners to write, draw, and/or discuss the answer to this question:

"Which stories have a small animal as the main character?"

Main Input

1. Read '**Tiger's Terror**' to your learners.

2. Ask your learners if this story reminds them of another story where a small animal scares big ones away by inviting an even bigger animal to walk with them. Listen to the justifications for every answer, as nothing should be 'wrong'.

If your learners do not connect this story to *The Gruffalo*, prompt them to do so using the following questions, perhaps adding that this story reminds you of one of your favourite books...

"Can you think of another story that is set in a 'deep dark wood'?"

"In which stories is there a small main character who has a long tail?"

"Which story has a character who goes on a journey and meets lots of different creatures wanting to eat them?"

"Which character who lives in the deep dark wood has purple prickles all over his back?"

If you have a copy of The Gruffalo, reveal it with enthusiasm when your learners make the connection, or when you decide to excitedly share 'the secret'. Take time to explore the similarities.

Independent Activity

Set your learners the challenge of retelling the story by swapping the fox for a different small animal, and swapping the tiger for a different big animal. The children can use copies of the stories if this would help them.

The animals can be modern, prehistoric (e.g. dinosaurs), or fictitious (e.g. 'Massive-O-Saurs'). You can leave your learners to attempt this activity individually, in pairs, or in groups.

Scaffold: Use the image prompts if needed.

There's more...

Plenary

Invite your learners to perform their stories for each other. *NB: You can also model this by letting a learner tell you their story, then you perform it to all your learners as a whole.*

Optional Extra

Offer your learners the chance to record their 'new' stories using writing and/or drawing.

Check In

Talk To Your Partner:

"What have you learnt today?"

Encourage your learners to share their thoughts, but remember: *there's no need to give away the Learning Objective in these lessons.*

Lesson A7:
Behind the Scenes

Julia Donaldson makes no secret of the fact that she based the story of *The Gruffalo* on this Chinese folk tale (albeit not the version here – *this* version of the Chinese original has been penned a good two decades after Julia sent her mouse into the deep dark wood...). But while this is often noted by educators and parents with a passing interest, it is rarely shared with *The Gruffalo*'s target audience, i.e. younger readers and listeners.

As a result, most young story lovers live with the misconception that *The Gruffalo* arose entirely from the genius that is Julia Donaldson.

Let us quickly clarify: we are not trying to downplay or deflate Julia's genius! Her adaptation is witty, fun, and enthralling, everything you need in a book to instil a love of story in youngsters – something *The Gruffalo* has achieved with unparalleled effect, along with her many other joyous works. And of course, Julia is a master of wordplay. If you use the Recyclable **Fun on the Page** lesson with *The Gruffalo* (which you absolutely should), your learners will be easily immersed in the delight of Donaldson's talent.

However, keeping your learners ignorant of *The Gruffalo*'s origins robs you of the chance to reveal Donaldson's important place in the transmission of stories over time – and so you lose an incredible opportunity to stimulate their interest in reading more widely. Younger generations often ask to hear the same story again and again, knowing it will bring them pleasure – it's like a security blanket. But if you prove to them that they can find something both new and similar *at the same time*, they'll gradually come to appreciate *and crave* the new as much as the old.

Moreover, when you come to look at creative writing with your learners, if they view Donaldson as being the sole originator of a timeless tale like *The Gruffalo*, you increase the risk that they see book writing as an ability of such high magnitude that they could never possibly achieve it themselves. Many may *aspire* to it, but eventually give up when they just can't seem to produce an original idea that excites the interest of others.

Your learners should be aware that it's not just OK to rely on old stories for inspiration, it's an absolute given! Julia Donaldson, Michael Rosen, Roald Dahl and Shakespeare (as we'll see later in this book), and of course Walt Disney wouldn't be the household names they are today without the use they made of proven crowd-pleasers from the past.

And of course, mentioning as much to your learners highlights some of the fortune on offer from being well-read...

There's more on this subject in the lessons from Volume B (along the Upper Pathway) – but for now, you should find that this lesson alone generates great wonder and excitement among your learners.

Lesson A8:
Story Links (II)

Learning Objective	**Success Criteria**
What will your learners 'learn', not 'do'?	*What must the learners do to be successful?*
• How the connections between books can encourage us to move from one book to another.	• Find books that link to the stories we have looked at so far. • (Optional) Understand and use the Opening technique in storytelling.

Resources

- 'Story Match' worksheet for the Starter.
- 'Book Finder' worksheet for the Independent Activity. *NB: You may wish to make this A3 to give your learners enough room to record their findings with drawings.*

Either…

- gather an assortment of children's books containing references to forests, shoes, lost items, tigers, foxes, and terror

or…

- arrange to deliver this lesson in a library – school library, local library, or bus.

Preparation

- Make sure you are familiar and confident in the use of the Opening technique mentioned in **Chapter 6** of this book.
- Find two contrasting examples for you to model during the Main Input.

Starter – *"Do Now!"*
Hooks into learning

Give the 'Story Match' worksheet to your learners and encourage them to match the correct summary to each story. You may choose to make this a timed challenge, and/or spend some time reviewing their answers afterwards.

Prior Knowledge Check

Talk To Your Partner:

"What are your favourite words from the stories we have read so far? Be ready to share *your partner's* choice."

Main Input

Put your learners in teams, hand each team a copy of the worksheet for recording, then **challenge** them to find and record as many books as possible that contain words from the groups on the worksheet. Highlight that these words link to the three stories '**Through the Forest**', '**One Lost Slipper**', and '**Tiger's Terror**'.

As with Lesson A4, **advise** your learners that pictures can give us clues to the words that might be on the page – but *only clues*. **Model** two contrasting examples (refer back to Lesson A4 for *our* example).

Let your learners know that there will be a prize if *every* team gets a score of at least 6 (for ages 4–5), 9 (for ages 5–7), or 12 (for ages 7+). **NB: You know your learners best, so ensure that the goal is achievable for all of them.**

Independent Activity

Your learners search the selection of books available in their teams.

After *at least* 10 minutes, end the challenge.

Each team calculates their points, scoring...

- one point for each book that definitely includes one of the words "woods", "forest", or "trees".

- two points for each book that definitely includes one of the words "shoe", "slipper", or "lost".

- three points for each book that definitely includes one of the words "tiger", "fox", or "terror".

Every team needs to hit the target. If a group is struggling, encourage learners who have already found the words to support those who haven't.

There's more...

Plenary

1. Encourage your learners to get excited about their prize: you're going to read their choice of book to them right now! Their choices must come from the books they've found during the Main Activity.

2. Your learners vote on the story to have read to them.

3. Read their chosen story aloud and use the Opening technique before any instance of a word from the worksheet, encouraging your learners to join in with that word and then cheer.

Optional Extra

Split your learners into small groups to read one of the books to each other, encouraging them to use the Opening technique modelled in the Plenary.

Check In

Talk To Your Partner:

"What have you learnt today?"

Encourage your learners to share their thoughts, but remember: *there's no need to give away the Learning Objective in these lessons.*

Story Match!

Draw a line between each story summary and the correct title.

Summary A

A fox meets an animal who wants to eat him, but tricks them into thinking that everyone is scared of the fox.

Title A
'Through the Forest'

Summary B

A Greek girl becomes a slave in Egypt, but a falcon brings her to the attention of the prince.

Summary C

Several fairytale characters are found wandering between the trees...

Title B
'One Lost Slipper'

Title C
'Tiger's Terror'

Score points for the books you find containing the words...

3 Points	2 Points	1 Point
Tiger	Shoe	Trees
Fox	Slipper	Forest
Terror	Lost	Woods

The REAL King of the Jungle

Based on an Indian folk tale
Adapted & written by Chip Colquhoun
Illustrated by Korky Paul

Some people once got very scared in the Indian jungle. The thick and twisty plants covering the bumpy ground were making their journey hard, and there weren't enough trees to hide from the blazing sun – so they felt more and more tired and dizzy.

That's why, when a lion burst out from a bush and surprised them, they panicked, and ran as fast as they could until they found a village.

Those people told everyone that the lion was huge and monstrous, and soon everyone said that the lion must be "the King of the Jungle".

But the animals in the jungle knew better. *They* knew that Jungle Lion was just an overgrown kitty-cat. Even Jungle Lion would say he'd only wanted to ask the people if they had a hairbrush for his knotted mane. Then he'd say, "Oh, you want the King Lion? You need to go to the African Savannah. There are no King Lions here."

You see, all the animals in the Indian jungle knew *exactly* who their king was – and any of them could tell you the story of how he became king in the first place...

At the start of this story, Tenduay the Leopard was smaller than Jungle Lion – but he had ten times the appetite. Being smaller also meant he could be swifter and sneakier through the thick and twisty plants blanketing the bumpy ground – and this made him better at catching animals for his food.

Much better. Tenduay had an antelope for breakfast, a monkey for a mid-morning snack, *two* antelopes for lunch, and a little red panda for afternoon tea. For each one there'd be a chase – **_swoosh!_** – a claw – **_swipe!_** – and lastly, Tenduay's jaws – **_chomp chomp chomp._**

For dinner, Tenduay chose between an elephant, a rhinoceros, or a the type of Indian cow known as a gaur. Sometimes he ate all three. **_Swoosh! Swipe! Chomp chomp chomp._**

For pudding, he decided between a python, a crocodile, or a duck. Sometimes he devoured all three. **_Swoosh! Swipe! Chomp chomp chomp._**

Finally, for supper, he selected from a hare, a pangolin, or a loris. Sometimes he gorged upon all three. **_Swoosh! Swipe! Chomp chomp chomp._**

TeTenduay's greed soon made the jungle look very untidy indeed. There weren't as many antelopes, hares, or gaurs to eat the plants covering the ground, so they grew from thick and twisty to something even worse: dense and tangled. And since there were fewer elephants, rhinos, or lorises to eat the leaves, the trees got so heavy that they bent towards the ground. Some even snapped and fell over.

With a shortage of red pandas and pangolins to munch on the bugs, there were so many creepy-crawlies wriggling and skittering around that everyone was itching terribly. And with a dearth of monkeys and ducks to spread seeds, there weren't enough new trees and plants to replace the dying ones. Lots of dead plants meant even more skittering bugs – like beetles, worms, and woodlice.

But that wasn't all. After eating most of his food, Tenduay left his leftovers hanging from the branches of trees – so he could come back later for seconds. This meant raw meat dangled all around the jungle – and *that* meant loads of flies buzzing around too.

Something had to be done. One day, all the jungle animals met up to discuss the matter – all except Tenduay. They met immediately after a heavy rain shower, because they knew Tenduay wouldn't be around. Tenduay *really* didn't like getting wet.

Being the largest animal there, Elephant spoke first. "Friends of the jungle," she said. We all know Tenduay the Leopard is eating far too much, and the jungle we call home is suffering."

Monkey interrupted. "But what can we do? None of us can fight Tenduay. Me and Hare are too small. You and Rhino are big, but too slow. Gaur and Antelope are just the right size, but they don't have the right teeth for fighting."

Red Panda was nervously watching Lion and the carnivorous reptiles. "What about Lion? *He* has the right teeth…"

Lion slowly shook his head. "We lions don't have the energy. Tenduay has been eating so much, he's taken most of the food from us – so we are all weak."

"The same is true for us," Crocodile added. "How do you think Tenduay has been able to sneak up and eat us for pudding?"

"But Gaur and Antelope have long horns," Python said. "Surely *they* can fight Tenduay?"

Gaur shook her head sadly. "Tenduay is too fast for us. We just have to face it: Tenduay is going to destroy our entire habitat."

"No," Elephant stated firmly. "Tenduay has to understand that if the jungle dies, we *all* die – including him. We must make a deal with him. Here's what I suggest…"

Elephant explained her idea. The other animals were shocked and scared at first, but soon they all agreed: there was no other way.

Elephant then trumpeted a loud call for Tenduay through her trunk.

Tenduay went along. He wasn't scared of all the animals standing together. He knew he could kill them all if he had to. "What's this all about?" he asked. "Hurry up. I'm getting hungry…"

Elephant spoke firmly. "Tenduay, your greed is killing the jungle. Look around: the grass is getting too long, the trees are getting too heavy, no new plants are growing, and everywhere is crawling with bugs and flies."

Tenduay shrugged. "So? That's not my problem. My only problem is what I'm having for lunch."

But Elephant remained resolute. "Both those problems are the same, Tenduay. If the jungle dies, you won't *have* any lunch."

That made Tenduay pause. If he couldn't get lunch in the jungle, he would have to move home. And then he might have to fight some of the other big cats – like the strongest of all: Tiger…

Irritated, Tenduay growled. "What do you want me to do, then?"

Elephant gave one last look to the other animals. They all nodded, so she told him, "From now on, you won't need to chase us. We will come to you. At midday every day, one of us will meet you at the giant mahua tree by the watering hole – and you can eat that animal.

"We will draw bamboo shoots to choose a new animal for you each day. Because you won't have to hunt us, one animal should be enough – and that will allow the jungle to recover.

"Do you agree?"

Tenduay thought about this a moment, then looked at all the animals one by one. They were all trying to look brave, but Tenduay could see them all shaking – even Lion.

So Tenduay grinned. "Yes, I agree – on two conditions. First, you must send *three* animals each day—"

"But—" Elephant tried to interrupt.

Tenduay quickly held up a paw to shut her up. "*One* for me to eat, one to give me a song or a story, and another to give me a wash. If I can't hunt, I'll need some other way to have fun – and if you want me to save energy, I can't wash myself."

Elephant looked around at the other animals. They all shrugged nervously. She looked back at Tenduay and said, "Fine. And your other condition?"

Tenduay's grin vanished, and he growled, "*Do not* be late. If one of you arrives so much as a *minute* after midday, I'll eat *every single one of you!* And this jungle can disappear forever…"

The animals flinched, and stared in frightened silence – until, at last, Elephant nodded. Then Crocodile nodded, then Gaur – and soon, everyone had nodded.

"We will never be late," Elephant assured Tenduay. "We all want the jungle to survive."

With that, the animals all went their separate ways – and Tenduay went to the giant mahua tree by the watering hole.

The next morning, the animals gathered again. Elephant held up a bunch of bamboo shoots in her trunk. Each animal took one with their eyes shut, then held them out to see who had taken the shortest.

Gaur held the shortest bamboo. "Oh well," she said. "I guess I'm getting eaten today."

Antelope held the next shortest bamboo. "I hope Tenduay likes my song," she said.

Red Panda held the next shortest. "Uck! I have to wash that stinky creep? I hope I don't ruin the shine on my lovely red fur…"

So Gaur, Antelope, and Red Panda rushed to the watering hole to get there for midday. Gaur and Antelope had strong, sturdy legs to travel steadily on the bumpy ground, so *they* wouldn't be late. And Red Panda was small and nimble to scurry through the dense and tangled plants. *He* wouldn't be late either.

Sure enough, they arrived in time for midday. Tenduay immediately set upon Gaur with a…? **_Swoosh! Swipe! Chomp chomp chomp._**

Then Tenduay lay back and listened to Antelope's song, while Red Panda scrubbed the sweat and mud from his fur.

The next morning, the animals gathered yet again. Elephant held up another clump of bamboo shoots in her trunk. Each animal took one at random, then compared them to see who had taken the shortest.

Elephant held the shortest bamboo. "Oh well," she said. "I guess it's my turn today."

Monkey held the next shortest. "I'm sure I can think of a story Tenduay will like," she said.

Duck held the next shortest. "Washing isn't so bad for me," he said. "I'm used to water!"

So Elephant, Monkey, and Duck rushed to the watering hole to get there for midday. Elephant had strong, sturdy legs that were twice the size of Antelope's – so *she* certainly wouldn't be late. Monkey swung through the trees to get there. *She* wouldn't be late either. Duck just swam along the river. There was no chance of *him* being late.

Sure enough, they all arrived in time for midday. Tenduay immediately set upon Elephant with a…? **_Swoosh! Swipe! Chomp chomp chomp._**

Then Tenduay lay back and listened to Monkey's story, while Duck used his feathers to wipe the sweat and mud from Tenduay's fur.

The next morning, the animals gathered once more. Elephant (a different elephant, of course) held up another assortment of bamboo shoots in her trunk. Each animal took one at random, then contrasted them to see who had taken the shortest.

Loris held the shortest bamboo. "Aw," he said. "I didn't plan to be eaten today. But oh well, it's all for the good of the jungle."

Crocodile held the next shortest bamboo. "I'm no good at singing *or* storytelling," she said. "I hope Tenduay won't mind me drumming…"

Python held the next shortest. "How am I supposed to wash him without any arms?" she wondered out loud. "Oh well. I suppose I'll have to find a way."

So Loris, Crocodile, and Python started on their way to the watering hole to get there for midday. Both Crocodile and Python moved fastest in water, so they both set off along the river. *They* wouldn't be late.

Loris, though, wasn't used to travelling fast in the sun. He usually stayed close to the trees, so he could always hide in the shadows – but to reach the watering hole, he had to traverse some treeless plains.

The sunlight dazzled his big round eyes, making it hard to see where he was going. Whenever he stopped to look, he realised he'd gone round in a circle! And it was a long way for his little legs. Soon he was dizzy, weary, and worried.

He was even more worried when he realised that the sun was in the centre of the sky. That meant it was midday! He was going to be late…!

He tried to move faster. At last, he spotted the giant mahua tree sticking up from the horizon. He rushed to it as fast as he could.

When Loris arrived at the watering hole, he found Tenduay there all alone.

"Oh," Loris said. "Where are Crocodile and Python?"

"They're here…" Tenduay replied calmly – then boomed, "…*in my* **belly!**"

Tenduay began to circle Loris, sneering, "You are *very* late, Loris! You know what that means? It means I now have to eat everyone in the jungle, and it's all *your* fault. *You* will be responsible for the death of the whole jungle! And I'll start with you…"

Loris may have had slow legs, but his mind worked fast. "Wait!" Loris said quickly. "It's the leopard's fault, not mine!"

Tenduay paused. "The leopard's fault? You're saying it's *my* fault?! Why you–"

"Not *you*, Tenduay," Loris replied hastily. "The *other* leopard! The leopard I met on my way here!"

Tenduay frowned. "*Another* leopard? *What* other leopard? I'm the only leopard in this jungle."

"You were," Loris agreed, "but as I made my way over here, I met another one. He threatened to eat me, so I told him I was on my way to meet you. That made him laugh, and he said you must be a weak leopard if you won't even hunt for your food."

"*What?!*" The orange fur on Tenduay's face began to turn red.

Loris nodded. "That's what I said! I told him you could catch *all* the animals in our jungle if you wanted! But he didn't believe me, and told me to bring you to him so he could challenge you – to a test of brawn."

"A test of what?" Tenduay asked.

"Brawn," Loris repeated. "I've never heard that word before either, but I *think* it means he wants to fight you to work out who's best."

Tenduay roared with rage, then got behind Loris. "Very well then!" he said. "Take me to this other leopard! I'll show *him* who's king around here…!"

"Th-th-th-this way…"

Loris took Tenduay along the riverbank. His mind was still running ten times as fast as his legs. His lie had got him this far – but how would he get away from Tenduay?

Tenduay growled impatiently. "Can't you go any faster?"

"I'm trying to remember the way," Loris replied apologetically.

Suddenly, Loris saw a cave beside the river. He pointed. "There! He went in there…!"

With another snarl, Tenduay leapt over Loris and ran to the cave. "Come out, coward!" he called. "Show yourself, phoney!"

There was no reply.

Tenduay peered into the cave…

…and there, looking up at him from below, was the other leopard.

Tenduay ROARED! – a thunderous bellow!

At exactly the same time, the other leopard roared back. He was definitely ready for a fight!

Well, thought Tenduay. *If it's a fight he wants, a fight he'll get!*

Tenduay thought quickly. The other leopard was almost exactly the same size as he was – with exactly the same markings too, in fact – but Tenduay had an advantage: he was higher up. With the other leopard below him, Tenduay could jump and land on the other leopard with all his claws – and have help from all his weight!

So Tenduay yelled, "Here I come, fiend!"

Tenduay *pounced* – and the other leopard pounced at exactly the same time.

Yes: *exactly* the same time.

Because it was exactly the same leopard.

Tenduay had been looking down at his own reflection in the water of a cave pool.

With a huge *SPLASH!*, Tenduay suddenly found himself surrounded by his biggest fear: *water!* And he didn't know how to swim…!

Loris didn't stay to find out what happened next. Instead, he made his way back to the jungle to let all the other animals know how he'd tricked Tenduay.

Tenduay was never seen again – at least, not in *that* jungle. Perhaps he was too ashamed of his foolishness, and ran away.

But all of the other animals cheered for Loris and his quick wit. From that day on, Loris and his family never had to travel fast to get anywhere, because they never had to run from anyone. Even today, there aren't many animals who will dare attack a slow loris.

And all the animals agree that *Loris* is the *real* king of the jungle. He bested a predator five times his size!

Lesson A9:
What's Going to Happen? (I)

Learning Objective *What will your learners 'learn', not 'do'?*	**Success Criteria** *What must the learners do to be successful?*
• The fun of wondering that comes from beginning a story.	• Enjoy listening to a story. • Make predictions about what might happen next in a story.

Resources

- Photocopies of the final illustration from '**The REAL King of the Jungle**'.
- (Optional, depending on your learners) Photos of lesser known animals from the story (e.g. loris, red panda, pangolin).

Preparation

- Read the story of '**The REAL King of the Jungle**' in advance, so that you are aware of the content. Consider how you may use VOICE with your learners.

Starter – *"Do Now!"*
Hooks into learning

Instruct your learners:

> "Talk to a friend about / Draw pictures of / Write a list of animals you might find in the jungle."

Decide on which would be best for your learners, or give them the choice of how to complete this activity.

Main Input

1. Read '**The REAL King of the Jungle**' to your learners **no further than the three leopard claws** (🐾 🐾 🐾), pausing shortly after the introduction of each new animal to ask your learners,

    "Do you know what this animal looks like?"

    If *anyone* doesn't, take a moment to display and discuss the look of the new animal(s).

2. At the point of the three leopard claws (🐾 🐾 🐾), pause. Ask your learners to **predict** what might happen next.

Independent Activity

1. Before reading any further (past the claws, to the end of the story), split your learners into individuals/pairs/small groups, and give them a copy of the final illustration from the story.

2. Challenge them to use that illustration to figure out (predict) what happens next, then either write, draw, and/or act out their idea of the ending.

Plenary

- Share some of your learners' predictions for the ending.

- As a reward for their hard work, you should *offer* to read them the real ending to the story – and then, after receiving the inevitable expression of colossal desire, read it to them!

Check In

Talk To Your Partner:

"What have you learnt today?"

Encourage your learners to share their thoughts, but remember: *there's no need to give away the Learning Objective in these lessons.*

Lesson A9:
Behind the Scenes

By now, whatever their starting point, your learners should all be hugely enthusiastic for stories, feel comfortable indulging that enthusiasm in an educational setting, and have an understanding of the importance and usefulness of stories. They should also have come to firmly link the pleasure of storytelling with the use of books – *many* **books. You may find many more of your learners choosing to read independently of their own accord.**

At this stage, the biggest hurdle to such autonomous independent reading will likely be 'reading stamina' – your learners' willpower to press on through a book to enjoy the satisfaction of reaching the end. If you've used the Recyclable **'What a Story Needs'** lesson with every story since **'One Lost Slipper'**, you'll have given them ample chance to enjoy that satisfaction. This lesson is about encouraging them to make the investment that provides such a rewarding return: *imaginative* investment.

Imaginative Investment

By the time you reach those claw marks in the text, your learners will have created Tenduay, Loris, and all the other jungle inhabitants within their minds. We describe this as their *imaginative investment*.

We've used the concept of investment several times already to describe your learners' engagement with these lessons, but we haven't used the term arbitrarily. As we mentioned in the **Behind the Scenes** for **Lesson A2** (page 63), when your learners invest their imagination – be it to create a character in their mind's eye or a piece of hand art on a paper 'stone wall' – they *care* about what they're doing.

This shouldn't come as a surprise, because caring about your investment is true of *all* types of investment. If you invest money in a house, you care about that house. If you invest time in a relationship, you care about that person. Our imaginations are no different. When your learners invest their imaginative energies to create the characters travelling the perilous paths of a story, they care enough to want those characters to overcome those perils. So pause the story, and they'll naturally be left wondering what becomes of the characters they've created.

If left unchecked, though, that curiosity could easily dissipate as other distractions come along – be they other lessons, games in the playground, or the stories found in other media once they return home.

So instead, in this lesson you're going to *nurture* that curiosity, and give your learners the freedom to play with it. And, just as with earlier lessons, this will lead them to associate feelings of fun and satisfaction with the act of going through a story – thereby encouraging them to seek out even more stories.

What's more, by offering the *real* ending as a 'reward', you'll amplify the satisfaction they'll feel by following the characters through to the resolution – or, to return to our metaphor, you'll be adding 'interest' to their investment.

By combining these elements of heightened wonder mid-story and enhanced satisfaction *post*-story, you'll be helping your learners to fully experience the rewards of reading to the end every time. This will soon come to feel completely natural to them, because nurturing their wonder for story will also have nurtured their willpower and stamina for story.

Right! Now your learners are primed to pick up books of their own accord. There's just one last little piece of encouragement for you to give them...

Lesson A10:
What's Going to Happen? (II)

Learning Objective	**Success Criteria**
What will your learners 'learn', not 'do'?	*What must the learners do to be successful?*
• How the wonderment of stories turns into the pleasure of reading.	• Enjoy hearing stories. • Understand how the beginning of a story gives you clues about what might happen, in order to hook readers in.

Resources

- A table (either on a board or flipchart) with 3 columns – one headed "Book Title", another headed "What I know from the beginning", and the third headed "Why I want to read the rest".

- A worksheet version of this table for your learners.

- Photocopies of the first 2 pages from at least 3 books your learners are familiar with, and a sheet listing the titles of those books (for the Prior Knowledge Check).

- A photocopy of the first 2 pages from a book that your learners haven't yet been exposed to (for the Main Input). Chip & Korky's *Fables & Fairy Tales* series (also published by Epic Tales) is especially good for this activity.

- Photocopies of the first 2 pages from a range of possible 'class reads' (for the Independent Activity).

Starter – *"Do Now!"*
Hooks into learning

Instruct your learners:

> "Talk to your friend about a book you really enjoyed reading, and say why it was so good. Challenge your friend to read it and see what they think."

Prior Knowledge Check

Give your learners the copies of opening pages from stories they're familiar with, along with a copy of the list of titles, and **challenge** them to match each opening to the correct title.

Main Input

1. Read the start of any story *that your learners haven't yet been exposed to*. But, after just two pages, suddenly stop.
   NB: Any story from Chip & Korky's Fables & Fairy Tales *series will be perfectly suited to this activity.*

2. Pause to ask your learners if they want to hear more of the story. If *any* say yes, begin a discussion about what's giving them that desire. Encourage your learners to think about what they've learned from the story so far, and what they now want to know.

3. **Model** putting their thoughts on the table.

4. *Instead of* continuing to read, announce the 'Two-Page Challenge' (the Independent Activity).

Independent Activity

Individually, in pairs, or in small groups, your learners are to look at the first 2 pages of potential 'class reads', and note anything that's making them want to find out more.

Give each team a copy of the worksheet and the selection of opening pages.

Set a time limit for the challenge.

Plenary

Encourage your learners to share their findings with each other:

"Has anyone else given the same reasons to continue reading as you?"

"Does anyone else want/not want to read one of the books you would like to continue reading?"

Check In

Talk To Your Partner:

"What have you learnt today?"

Encourage your learners to share their thoughts, but remember: *there's no need to give away the Learning Objective in these lessons.*

HIGHLY RECOMMENDED Optional Extra!

Let your learners vote on which story should be the next class read – and use it!

NB: If a child wants to read a book that didn't get selected, encourage them to take it home to read independently/with their family, or read it during the school day.

Book Title	What I know from the beginning	Why I want to read the rest

Lesson A10:
Behind the Scenes

This lesson ends with you putting the choice of your next 'class read' into the hands of your learners. If this idea fills you with trepidation, remember: giving your learners control over what they study is a way of inviting their *investment* into that study. The result will be learners who are far more motivated, engaged, and focused.

But this choice isn't based simply on a title or a cover. It's based on two pages of text. Whether intentionally or subconsciously, the best children's authors saturate their first two pages with the neurological hooks we looked at in Section 1 – so before page 3, you should be able to tell that something isn't right (a Bad Thing), there's a character you can identify with (an Empathetic Main Character), and there's a reason behind the adventure ahead (an *expectation* of a Message, if not the Message itself). So by allowing your learners to make their choice after reading the opening pages of the available options, you're ramping up their excitement for the act of *continued* reading.

> **WE CANNOT RECOMMEND HIGHLY ENOUGH THIS METHOD FOR DECIDING YOUR NEXT CLASS READ!** It really can make the difference between (a) a class read that loses the interest of some or more of your learners along the way, or (b) a reading atmosphere that *oozes* with concentration, enthusiasm, and progress.

Plus, remember everything that's been said in this book about 'reading stamina'. The stories you've worked with so far, whichever Pathway you took to get here, have been relatively short – making it easy for your learners to quickly develop a taste for those neurological hooks, along with a sense of how stories move from set-up to crisis to resolution. Now you've used these lessons to fire up your learners' readiness to read for pleasure, they'll have the fortitude for *longer* stories – so include first pages from a range of chapter books, and you'll find your learners eagerly investing in a story to last the entirety of next term.

Whether you intend to continue with the stories in Volume B, to begin sharing some of Chip and Korky's *Fables & Fairy Tales*, or to move onto any other storybook for children, you should find that your learners have never been more willing to sit and listen to you read – *and* that they've never been more willing to pick up and explore a book in their own time...

STORY VOLUME B:
Upper

Huh, Part 2

Based on true archaeological findings
Written by Chip Colquhoun
Illustrated by Korky Paul

What I'm about to share with you is the most amazing second part to a story you will ever hear. It may not be your *favourite* second part to a story ever, but it really is amazing, it really is important, and it really *is* from a time when people like you and me lived in caves, a time when the land was covered in ice, and a time *just before* stories had kept people alive for**…?**

Forty thousand years.

And in some ways, this second part is even more amazing than the first, because it tells of the *Special Day* when a cave person had the *Two Most Incredible Thoughts Ever*.

Remember: back then, around **forty thousand years** ago, humans like you and me wore furry capes wrapped around their hairy bodies. They had big, bulging muscles. They were usually splattered with mud all over, because they hadn't invented showers yet. And one of these humans went by the name of Huh – which meant**…?**

"Oo, that's interesting."

Back then, around **forty thousand years** ago, Huh lived in a cave with his sisters Hmm and Oo, his cousin Wuh, and his uncle Duh. At night, all five of them cuddled together around their fire to keep warm.

If they didn't, they'd die.

You see, it was *very* cold back then, around **forty thousand years** ago. If you went out during the day, you'd soon have frost woven between your eyelashes, and icicles dangling from your nose – icicles which would soon fall off, though, from all your shivering.

But when the Sun went below the horizon and night began, the temperature would drop so low that no human being could survive outside – no matter how thick their furry cape. If you didn't get back to your cave in time to huddle around a fire with your fellow humans… you'd be dead.

That's why Huh the human and

his family, all clothed in fur, would head back to their cave the moment they saw the Sun beginning to go down. They made sure they never travelled too far when searching for food, and always remembered how long their journey had been – so they knew how long they would need to get back.

Just outside their cave was a forest. On the day *before* the Special Day when the *Two Most Incredible Thoughts Ever* were about to be made, Huh walked in a straight line through the forest, hunting for a wild pig to catch for their evening meal. He walked for ten minutes... twenty minutes... thirty... a whole *forty minutes*, and still he hadn't found any food. Had they caught the last wild pig near their cave?

Forty-five minutes away from the cave, Huh found himself at a field of grasses and small bushes. He had walked right out the other side of the forest! None of his family had walked this far, not since the ice had come to cover the land. Huh knew he needed to remember how long it had taken him to get there, which was—

"Huh!" he said suddenly – which meant...? "Oo, that's interesting!" Because, on one of those small bushes, Huh noticed a bird poking its beak into a small hard shell among the branches.

Getting closer, Huh found many more small hard shells among the branches of those shrubs. Some were closed, like little round stones, but some had a gap he could squeeze his fingers into – and *snap!* He broke them apart, and found a soft lump inside.

He sniffed it, then licked it – then popped it in his mouth and bit. The lump broke apart in his mouth with a sound a little like 'ut'.

Huh smiled and said, "Huh!" – which meant...? "Oo, that's interesting!" Because of the sound it had made, he decided to call it an *ut*.

Huh began walking along the edge of the forest, breaking off a few branches of uts as he went to drag along behind him. When the ut shrubs stopped, Huh shivered from the cold, which made him think to look up and check the time – but—

"Huh!" he said suddenly, which meant...? "Oo, that's interesting!" And he grinned, because he had caught sight of a *berry bush*.

He knew his sisters, his cousin, and his uncle would all like some sweet, juicy berries after eating their uts – it would make dinner doubly delicious! So he stayed a bit longer to break off some branches of berries too.

After a while, he shivered again. It was getting even colder – and Huh stopped still.

He gulped, and looked up to see where the Sun had got to.

It was forty-five minutes from the horizon!

Huh now had a choice: keep going around the forest until he got back to his cave, or go *through* the forest back to his cave.

Which would *you* have chosen?

Remember: if you had chosen to go *around* the forest, the Sun would have gone below the horizon before you got back to your cave – and the temperature would have dropped so low that no human could survive. Huh remembered that too, so he went through the forest straight back to his family's cave. True, he *might* have found another cave somewhere around the forest, maybe with another family who would let him cuddle with them around a fire – but Huh didn't even *think* to risk it. Going straight home meant he was sure to survive!

This wasn't especially clever, by the way. There are lots of animals who would have done exactly the same as Huh. Even today, there are *snails* who use the Sun to decide when to go home. Huh was being about as clever as a snail – but he didn't mind as long as he was alive.

Because Huh wasn't looking for wild pigs this time, he actually got back to the cave in *less* than forty-five minutes. Hmm and Oo were already there, and had started a fire burning, so the cave was already warming up nicely. Huh showed his sisters the new food he'd found, which he'd called**…?** *Uts*. He revealed the berries as well, and both his sisters grinned.

All their grins disappeared as Wuh suddenly dashed in. He looked *terrified*.

"Buh, Duh!" said Huh, which meant, "Where's Uncle Duh?" Wuh and Duh had gone out hunting together.

Wuh wiped tears from his eyes, then quickly explained what had happened. Wuh and Duh had both been searching for wild pigs in the forest when they'd noticed the Sun starting to drop towards the horizon. Just as they turned to head home, a *great beast* had burst from the trees!

It was *huge!* It had enormous rippling muscles, giant leathery hands, and glistening long sharp teeth! Before Wuh or Duh could do anything, the beast leapt over to Duh, grabbed him with both its gigantic hands, and… and…

Wuh had to stop and wipe even

more tears from his eyes. At last, he finished his tale by saying they would never see their Uncle Duh again. The beast had eaten him. Wuh hadn't waited to see if the beast wanted pudding. He had turned and raced back to the cave as fast as he could, desperate to escape both the cold *and* the beast.

Huh and his sisters gathered round to hug Wuh. They stayed like that for the rest of the night, all clad in fur, the warmth of their hug and the heat from the fire once again protecting them from the freezing cold.

The next day was the *Special Day* – the day when a cave person would have the *Two Most Incredible Thoughts Ever*. But no-one knew that yet. Everyone just got on and did what they usually did.

For Huh, that meant going out in search of more food. The uts and berries had been tasty and satisfying, but they were all gone by the end of the night. A wild pig could feed them all for two or three days. Which would he find on this new day?

Huh walked a route around the forest this time, but he still didn't see any wild pigs. After a couple of hours or so, he found the ut shrubs from the day before. There were still several branches full of uts – so he broke off just a few more, and began dragging them along behind him.

Eventually he came to the berry bushes again – just as he'd hoped. He started snapping off a few of *those* branches too.

His body shivered a bit, which made him think to check where the Sun had got to…

…and it was again just forty-five minutes away from the horizon! Just like the day before!

Once again, Huh had a choice: keep going around the forest until he got back to his cave, or go *through* the forest back to his cave.

Which would you have chosen *this* time?

Remember: if you had chosen to go *around* the forest, the Sun would have gone below the horizon before you got back to your cave – and the temperature would have dropped so low that no human could survive. Huh remembered that too – but something in his mind was stopping him from just going straight through the forest.

What did he think might be in the forest?

The *beast* that had eaten Uncle Duh! If Huh went through the forest, he might *not* survive this time. He might get eaten by the same monster!

But what Huh didn't realise was that he had just had the *first* Most Incredible Thought Ever. Did you spot it?

He had remembered a memory... that *wasn't even his!*

Huh had never seen that beast. He hadn't been there when Uncle Duh got eaten. All of that was *Wuh's* memory, not Huh's.

And yet, in that moment, Wuh's memory was popping up in Huh's mind – all because Wuh had shared that story with him.

You might not think this is all that incredible. That's probably because you do it all the time. But when Huh remembered Wuh's memory, a memory that wasn't his own... That was the first time this had *ever* happened – the first time in the history of *the world!*

And it was a Most Incredible Thought because, right then, that thought was the thing stopping Huh from walking into the forest and getting eaten.

But that Incredible Thought hadn't saved Huh's life. Not yet. He was still on the edge of the forest, remember. If he stayed there, or if he tried going home *around* the forest... he'd be dead! The Sun would go below the horizon before he got back to his cave, and the temperature would drop so low that no human could survive.

So what could he do? Knowing that he only had forty-five minutes to get home, and knowing that there could be a people-eating monster waiting for him in the forest... how could he make sure he got back to his cave alive?

Huh made a plan. And I'll be honest: I don't know what plan he made. I wasn't there, and all record of Huh's plan has been lost. After all, this was how long ago...? **Forty thousand years** ago. That's a lot of time for stories to go missing.

But what plan would *you* have made? How would *you* have got back to the cave alive if you were a Stone Age caveperson like Huh?

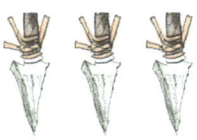

Yes – how would *you* have guaranteed your survival?

By climbing and swinging through the trees to keep away from wherever the beast was lurking?

By covering yourself in mud and leaves to give yourself a disguise?

By using something around you to make a weapon?

By lighting a few branches on fire to keep yourself warm as you walked around the forest – or maybe even using *that fire* as a weapon against the beast?

Something else?

Huh could have used any of those ideas. Like I said, I don't know what plan he made. All I know is that he *did* make a plan, and *that* meant he had just taken the *second* Most Incredible Thought Ever.

He had thought about something *which hadn't happened yet*.

You might not think this is so incredible, because you do it all the time. You probably find it easy to think about what might happen on your next birthday, or the next time you visit your best friend, or the next time you play your favourite game. But when Huh made a plan for what might happen if he met the beast, something which hadn't happened yet, that was again the first time this had *ever* happened – another first in the history of *the world!*

These Two Incredible Thoughts had given Huh a new superpower – which was? *Imagination.*

And hey! When you were thinking of *your* plan just now – how *you* would have survived if *you* had been in Huh's position – *you* were using that superpower too!

This superpower kept Huh alive. We know it did, because Huh returned to his cave and taught the rest of his family how to use it too. Huh and his fur-clad family shared this superpower with their other human friends as well, until they were *all* using Imagination – to catch food, to avoid *being* food, and to think of ways they could stay alive even though the climate was changing.

Thanks to Huh and his friends using Imagination and sharing stories, the human race survived – for another...? **Forty thousand years.**

And as we saw when you thought of how *you* would have survived in Huh's position, every human – I mean *every* human – still has that superpower today.

Even you.

So with *you* in the world, who knows? Maybe the human race will be able to survive into the future for yet another...?

Forty thousand years!

Lesson B1:
The Most Important Invention *Ever!* (II)

Important Note

Your learners must have heard the story of 'Huh' from earlier in this book to fully access, appreciate, and benefit from the learning in this lesson.

Learning Objective
What will your learners 'learn', not 'do'?

- How stories make us really great thinkers.

Success Criteria
What must the learners do to be successful?

- Help a character overcome a problem.
- Enjoy a story.
- Share their ideas about a text.

Resources

- Art and/or writing materials.

Preparation

- Read the story of '**Huh, Part 2**' in advance so you are aware of the content. Consider how you may use VOICE with your learners.

Starter – *"Do Now!"*
Hooks into learning

Instruct your learners:

"Discuss, draw, or write about what you can remember from the story of 'Huh'."

Prior Knowledge Check

Sequence events from the story of '**Huh**' from **Volume A**.

NB: You may need to re-read this story to your learners.

Main Input

1. Read the story of '**Huh, Part 2**' to your learners altogether, up to the three flints (🔥🔥🔥). Take time to enjoy the discussions prompted by the text.

2. Pause at the three flints (🔥🔥🔥) to thoroughly discuss the question,

   "How would *you* have got back to the cave alive if you were a Stone Age caveperson like Huh?"

3. Encourage your learners to share their ideas. If you have a learning wall, you could record this there as a mind map to support them in their Independent Activity.

Independent Activity

As individuals, pairs, or small groups, set your learners the task of writing, drawing, and/or performing their ideas for how Huh could get safely through the forest.

Plenary

Read the remainder of the story to your learners.

Check In

Talk To Your Partner:

"What have you learnt today?"

Encourage your learners to share their thoughts, but remember: *there's no need to give away the Learning Objective in these lessons.*

Lesson B1:
Behind the Scenes

If you began this book in Section 1, you took a test. So long as you completed that test without breaking any of the rules, you proved for yourself the powers of story-led learning. But you *also* proved this to be *your* power – *you* remembered information gleaned for the very first time, and *you* filled in missing details using *your* imagination.

This lesson is your chance to provide the same 'Aha!" moment for your learners. As they progress through the story, they'll catch themselves doing exactly what Huh was doing – thereby proving that they do indeed have these same superpowers.

Non-Contributors

Even if a learner doesn't contribute to the discussion, the intrinsic nature of the imagination means that they'll almost certainly be sharing in Huh's memory (or rather, Wuh's), and also inventing means of surviving the trek through the forest. However, if they don't contribute, they *may* be less inclined to believe they do indeed share the superpower.

This is why you'll break up your reading of the story with an activity that sees your learners working individually, in pairs, or in small groups: by doing so, you increase the opportunity for them to *feel* themselves being creative. Just be sure that, when you come to read the ending, you celebrate *everyone* for their creative efforts, whether they shared their ideas *or not*.

Lesson B2:
We Need Stories

Important Note

Your learners must have completed Lesson A6 from Volume A, as your learners will only fully access, appreciate, and benefit from the learning in this lesson if they have already heard the story of **'One Lost Slipper'** and have an understanding of the importance of **'The Bad Thing'** in stories.

Learning Objective
What will your learners 'learn', not 'do'?

- How to identify the *second* essential element of a good story: the *Message*.

Success Criteria
What must the learners do to be successful?

- Understand the Message in a given story.
- Think about what they learn from stories they already know well.
- Share their ideas.

Resources

- Photocopies of the Survival Test worksheet.

Starter – *"Do Now!"*
Hooks into learning

Instruct your learners:

"Discuss, draw, or write about what you can remember from the story of **'One Lost Slipper'**."

Prior Knowledge Check

Remind your learners how Huh learned a lesson from his cousin's story which helped him to survive, then invite them to discuss this question:

"What lessons did *you* learn from *Huh's* story?"

Main Input

1. Ask your learners to discuss these questions in relation to '**Huh, Part 2**':

   "What did we learn about the power of stories?"

   "What did Wuh's story help Huh to do?"

   "Once Huh got the power of imagination, what was he able to do?"

2. After identifying the importance of stories for helping us survive, remind your learners of '**One Lost Slipper**' and ask them to think of any ways in which *that* story could help someone survive.

   *Steer the conversation towards identifying whether the story was actually about Rhodopis staying alive, or whether it was about her **living happily**.*

3. Ask your learners to think about, and discuss, these questions in relation to '**One Lost Slipper**':

   "Was Rhodopis' life actually in danger at any point?"

   "If Rhodopis wasn't in danger of dying in her story, what did she actually *get* from the story?"

   "What good came from Rhodopis' story?"

   "Are there any other ways the story shows us how to live more happily?"

4. Ultimately, use '**One Lost Slipper**' to steer your learners towards identifying that...

   "Surviving isn't just about staying alive,
   it's about thriving and being happy!"

Independent Activity

Invite your learners to think of their favourite stories (from books, films, TV shows, even video games) and record the messages in those stories for how we can "stay alive, thrive, or be happy".

There's more...

Plenary

- Invite your learners to share their thoughts and create a class record of messages from stories they know for how we can "stay alive, thrive, or be happy".

Check In

Talk To Your Partner:

> "What have you learnt today?"

Encourage your learners to share their thoughts, but remember: *there's no need to give away the Learning Objective in these lessons.*

Survival Test!

How does this story help us to stay alive, thrive, or be happy?

Story Title

Lesson B2:
Behind the Scenes

When you first use this lesson, you'll begin by capitalising on your learners' enjoyment of the 'Huh' and 'One Lost Slipper' stories. Then you'll compound that enjoyment by allowing them to consider the significance of their own favourite stories – from whatever media, be it books, films, video games, etc. And so, as with Lesson A1, you'll be mixing sheer pleasure with the very intrinsic elements that draw us to stories in the first place – making stories irresistible.

Of course, as stated elsewhere, our goal throughout these lessons is to make stories *from books* irresistible – and that's one reason we made this lesson Recyclable. By using this same format whenever you consider a new book, for shared or independent reading, you're helping your readers to connect the process with their experience of enjoyment.

But the main reason for this being a Recyclable lesson is because it introduces them to that second key element of all good stories: the *Message*.

Never fear that understanding the key elements of stories will put your learners off *enjoying* the stories. The reality is completely the opposite. Remember our walking analogy: when keen walkers learn the health benefits of their leisurely pastime, they grow even more enthusiastic about it. Your phonics and comprehension lessons are the equivalent of teaching the mechanics of walking, i.e. 'one foot in front of the other'. Revealing the importance of story for helping us stay alive, thrive, or be happy? That's the icing on the cake.

And just like keen walkers get physically fitter, thereby improving their ability to walk further and faster, and get even *more* enjoyment from the pursuit, so too will combining the pleasure of reading with its neurological benefits help to increase the potency of both. The better your learners become at spotting Bad Things and Messages, the faster their curiosity will be sparked by a book – and so the sooner they'll be hooked.

"What if a learner wants to use the Survival Test on a work of non-fiction?"

As discussed in our Introduction, the benefits of reading for pleasure are most prevalent when reading books *designed* for pleasure – the 'fiction effect' detected by Jerrim and Moss.

However, at this stage, we're aiming to cultivate your learners' enthusiasm for books and stories, and allowing them to feel ownership over the experience is a major part in that. So if a learner wishes to explore how a history book or science book improves their chances of staying alive, thriving, or being happy, let them have at it. Chances are both they *and you* will come away with heaps of insights!

If they want to go down this route but get stuck, try asking them why they *enjoy* that book. It's likely they picked a book that matches their interests – e.g. a book on dinosaurs because they enjoy learning more about dinosaurs, or a programme on space because they enjoy learning more about space. In other words, this medium is helping them to 'be happy' by increasing their knowledge. That's a golden opportunity to help them realise the pleasure that can arise simply from *learning!*

You never know – that may start to feed into their approach to other subjects too...

The Mountain Inside a Molehill

Based on a Norwegian folk tale
Adapted & written by Chip Colquhoun
Illustrated by Korky Paul

Sitting at the top of a tall blue mountain somewhere underground, Saul knew he was in the worst kind of trouble. He was exhausted, alone, and defeated. If only he had listened to his mum the other day…

That morning, he had woken up from the strangest dream, in which he'd seen a man who looked about a thousand years old. This old man had carried a walking stick, but he hadn't needed it. He had danced and hopped, while gleefully singing,

Oh what fun, this job I've done!
I snatched a girl from below the
    sun,
And down a hole, this girl I stole
Is now a slave to a big mean troll!

Then in return, so I did earn
A magic drink in a purple urn.
It makes my might a wondrous
    height
So I will win each and any fight!

I can't chop wood, but if I could,
I'd be the best in the
    neighbourhood.
And funny thing: this girl I sing
Is daughter to the queen and king!

Over breakfast, Saul described the dream to his mum. She looked up from the newspaper to listen to him, then looked back at the newspaper and said, "That *is* strange. *Very* strange."

She held the newspaper open so Saul could see it.

"Look here," she said. "It says the princess has been kidnapped, just like the old man sang in your dream. You know what that means, don't you?"

Saul gasped. "My dream is telling me to rescue the princess?!"

His mum blinked. "Don't be silly, you're just a boy. No, your dream is telling you we'll never need to buy another newspaper, because your dreams will tell us everything we need to know. Now go out and chop some wood for our fire, that's what you're good at."

Saul did indeed pick up the axe he used for chopping firewood. But instead of doing as his mum had said, he carried his axe and set off through the forests of Norway where they lived, heading in the direction of the palace.

He was just about to enter the city gates when a man in armour marched out. Saul had never seen knights in real life, so he stopped and stared at the man's bulging body.

The knight saw Saul staring, and laughed. "I expect you want to be like me one day!"

"Yes," Saul replied, "and I will be soon!"

That made the knight laugh louder. "I don't think so, boy. You've still got a lot of growing up to do."

But Saul shook his head. "Oh no. I'm going to rescue the princess. I'll be a knight within a week!"

Now the knight stopped marching to look more carefully at Saul. He raised one eyebrow, then smiled and said, "Well then, you should know: they think the princess was kidnapped by a troll, and the king has sent me to rescue her. But usually it takes two knights to fight a troll: a captain like me, and a bait. Do you know what a 'bait' is, boy?"

Saul shook his head.

The captain replied, "Ah! A bait is the most important knight after captain! Would you like to be my bait?"

Saul nodded, eagerly: barely a day into his new adventure, and he was already a knight! He excitedly followed the captain into the Norwegian forest.

They searched the forest for a long time, but found no trace of trolls. Just as the Sun went down, they found a clear grassy patch between the trees.

"We'll rest here tonight," the captain said. "Can you fetch some firewood while I pitch a tent?"

"Sure!" Saul replied. "I'm good at chopping wood!"

Off Saul went to chop, smiling widely. He was only 10, but he was a knight already! And a *special* kind of knight, too: a 'bait'! He hummed a happy tune as he chopped.

However, when Saul got back to the cottage, he found the captain lying beside the tent, covered in bruises and rubbing his head.

"What happened?" Saul asked.

"It was so frightfully unexpected!" the captain replied. "This old man with a walking stick came round. He looked about a thousand years old, and begged me for a coin to buy some food. I gave him one, but he dropped it, and when I bent down to pick it up for him... *whack!* He began beating me with his stick! He was tenaciously tough – and before I could get up, he took *all* my money and ran off!"

Saul gasped. An old man beating up a knight? And a knight *captain* at that! "How horrible!" he said.

"Now we'll have to rest here tomorrow while I heal," the captain said with a sigh.

They ate and slept, and the next day they rested in the tent while the captain healed. While Saul sat, though, he kept wondering: there was something familiar about the captain's description of the old man...

Towards the evening, the captain said, "Right! Since we'll be here for another night, we need more firewood." Before Saul could say anything, he added, "You stay here and guard the tent. I'm a big hulking knight, so I should be the one chopping the trees."

With that, the captain marched into the forest with his sword. Saul just shrugged, sighed, and sat some more.

A short while later, a twig snapped behind him, and Saul looked around to see why.

Have you ever had one of those moments where something happens, and you're sure you've seen it before? Even though you know you couldn't have? That's what Saul felt as he saw an old man step into the grassy clearing. This old man seemed to be at least a thousand years old, and leaned on a wooden walking stick...

The elderly man grinned at Saul with toothless gums. "Dear lad," he said. "I don't suppose you could spare me a coin? I'm old and frail, see, and I have no talents – but with your coin I could buy a meal to save my life."

Those words prompted Saul to remember the words to a song...

I can't chop wood, but if I could,
I'd be the best in the neighbourhood.

So Saul said, "I'm very sorry. I want to help you, but I don't have any coins. I can give you a talent, though. How about I teach you how to chop wood?"

The old man's eyes opened

wide. "You'd do that? Oh, yes please! Why, then I'd be the bes– I mean… then I could earn my *own* coins!"

Together, Saul and the old man went a little way into the forest. Saul found a tall beech tree, then swung his axe into the tree with a *chnnk* (which is like a chunk, only deeper). He swung like that twice more, and the tree fell with a *thmmp* (which is like a thump, only heavier).

Saul took the man to one end of the fallen tree and said, "If you rest your head on the tree here, you'll get the best view of how I chop the trunk into logs. That's how my dad taught me."

Gratefully, the man rested his head on the fallen tree, his long white beard laying along the bark.

Saul raised his axe, swung the blade down…

…and with the chunkiest *CHNNK!*, he wedged the old man's beard between his blade and the bark!

It didn't matter how strong the old man was. He *might* have been able to pull himself away from the axe – but that would mean ripping out his beard, and he didn't like that idea. So instead, he begged Saul for his life.

"You can live," Saul said, "on one condition: you tell me how to find the princess."

"Yes yes!" the old man agreed quickly. "Under your tent you'll find a little mound made by a mole. At the top of that mound is a hole. Go down there and you'll find the mountain where the princess is imprisoned."

Saul frowned. "A mountain? In a molehill?"

"Yes!" the man confirmed, nodding sincerely – then grimaced, because nodding pulled painfully at his beard. "But be warned: to reach it, first you must pass the ice, the fire, and the dark!"

"Thank you!" Saul replied, then made to leave.

"Wait!" the old man called. "Won't you let me go?"

Saul smiled. "When I get back – so I know you haven't tricked me."

As soon as the captain returned, Saul told him what he'd learnt from the old man. Saul expected the captain to say "Well done!" or "Thank you!", but he didn't. Saul guessed knights just weren't used to saying "Well done" or "Thank you".

The captain *was* excited, though. Right away, he tore down the tent. Sure enough, there was a molehill, at the top of which was a hole. The captain used his sword to widen it.

When they peered down, though, neither of them could see anything. It seemed to go down forever!

The captain found some rope in his bag, then said, "It's my job to rescue the princess, so you should lower me down and stay here to pull us up. Only pull if I tug on the rope three times."

Then the captain wrapped one end of the rope around his waist and under his arms, and climbed into the hole. For a long time, Saul let the rope slip slowly through his fingers – until the rope suddenly jerked three times.

Saul quickly pulled it up.

The captain's head popped back out of the hole, his eyes wide and his face blue. "I-i-i-t's s-s-s-so c-c-c-cold-d-d-d..." he whimpered.

Saul stepped forward. "Can I try?" he said.

The captain agreed. First, though, Saul gathered a bunch of sticks. Only then did he wrap himself in the rope and climb through the hole...

The captain had only lowered Saul a little way when, suddenly, the air got so cold that Saul's saliva became ice cubes on his tongue!

But Saul had been expecting that. He just took one deep breath of the freezing air, then huddled deeper into his clothes.

Then, without warning, the air grew so hot that Saul's saliva began to boil!

But Saul had been expecting that, too. He just breathed out the icy air to cool his tongue, and held out his bunch of sticks. The sticks instantly burst into flame from the heat.

Lastly, the air went pitch black. This could have been terrifying – but Saul's bunch of burning sticks gave him light to see by.

At last, Saul felt ground under his feet. He unwrapped himself from the rope and looked around. In one direction, he saw a blue glow. *The sky!* he thought. *That must be where the princess is.* Off he set towards it.

As he got closer, though, Saul realised that the glow was *not* the sky – it was a mountain! A mountain made out of a bright, shimmering blue rock! It was beautiful... and it was *ginormous!* How did it fit in this hole?!

By the side of the mountain was a large wooden hut, which looked like it had been put together by someone who didn't know how to build a hut. Saul went over and poked his head through the door.

The first thing Saul noticed was the smell – like a gazillion Brussels sprouts. There was only one room, with two wooden chairs and a wooden table. One chair was massive, the kind a giant might sit in.

The other chair was normal size, and in it sat a princess, her face buried in her hands.

Saul coughed politely.

The princess' head snapped up. "Oh!"

"Excuse me, Princess," Saul said. "I'm sorry to disturb you, but I've come to rescue you. Do you mind if I take you home?"

The princess thought for less than half a quarter of a second. "I don't mind," she said, "but I don't know how you will. I'm chained to this table, you see, and a six-headed troll has the key. He'll be back any minute now – and you don't even have a sword to fight him with."

Saul knew she was right – but then he noticed a large sword by the fireplace. "I'll use that one," he said, and went over to pick it up.

But it wasn't just large – it was *heavy*, too heavy for Saul to lift. He sighed. Maybe he wouldn't rescue the princess after all.

Suddenly, though, he spotted something on the table that looked like a purple jug with no handle. The colour prompted Saul to remember some more words of a song…

Then in return, so I did earn
A magic drink in a purple urn.
It makes my might a wondrous
    height
So I will win each and any fight!

Saul thought that song had helped him a fair bit already, so he decided to give the drink a try. He went over and took a sip. It tasted like a mixture of honey and apple juice.

Then he went back to the sword, grasped the hilt…

…and this time, he picked it up easily!

The princess gasped – then smiled brightly. (Saul thought she had a beautiful smile.) But then she looked serious again, and said, "You mustn't be standing there when the six-headed troll comes in. He drinks that drink too, and he's bigger than you. You'll need to take him by surprise."

"How can I do that?" Saul wondered aloud.

"Hide under his chair," the princess said. "When he gets back, he'll sit there and ask me to scratch the icky hairs on all his heads. When I do that, he'll get sleepy – so when you hear me say 'Sweet dreams, dear dear dear dear dear dear,' that will be your chance to pop up and cut him down."

Saul thought the princess' plan was brilliant! (He thought the princess was brilliant too.) So he slid under the giant chair – just in time, too, because then the six-headed troll lumbered into the hut with feet like tree stumps.

Saul listened as the troll plonked itself in its chair, and dribbled the words, "Right, pinssess! Ratch me 'eads! *NAAAAWL!*"

(And yes: "dribbled the words". Saul could hear them splashing on the floorboards around him.)

"Yes, dear dear dear dear dear dear," the princess said, and Saul could hear the rattle of her chain as she moved from her seat to the troll. Then came a sound Saul had never heard before – a cross between chalk drawing on a blackboard, and thick wet mud slapping against a pig.

Saul's face crinkled. He couldn't imagine how disgusted the princess was feeling – she had the most revolting job!

Eventually, though, Saul thought he heard six little snores – and the princess whispered, "Sweet dreams, dear dear dear dear dear dear…"

Saul instantly rolled out from under the chair, and swept the sword through the air. It smoothly sliced through the troll's heads: *one-two-three-five-six*. The troll collapsed with a *thmmp*.

Saul dropped the sword and reached for the key on the troll's belt…

"*NO!*" cried the youngest princess…

…and the troll stood up! It still had one head left…! "*CMM 'ERE!*" it roared, and reached for Saul.

As a monstrous hairy fist clasped Saul's entire body, he felt sure his life was about to be crushed out of him…

…but then, with a *SHLRRPT!*, the troll's last head flew away from its neck.

The hand fell limp, and Saul clambered out to see the princess standing with the purple urn in one hand, the giant sword in her other hand, and juicy honeyey drink sloshed around her lips.

"Thank you!" Saul said. "That was fantastic!" (He thought the princess was fantastic too.)

"You're welcome," the princess replied. "Now let's get out of here quick, I don't want to spend another minute in this abominable place."

"Of course!" Saul replied. "Follow me."

On the way back to the rope, Saul chatted and laughed with the princess. He discovered she was the same age as him, she also enjoyed chopping firewood, and she'd also dreamt a strange dream recently. She was just about to describe her dream when she suddenly walked into the dangling rope and said, "Oh! Is this it?"

Saul grasped the rope to stop it swinging about. "Yep! Ladies first."

The princess let Saul wrap the rope around her. Before he could give the signal for the captain to pull her up, though, she said, "I haven't thanked you properly yet. I'm sure you'll be rewarded by my parents when we get home, but I want to thank you personally – so here..."

She unclipped her necklace, and passed it to Saul. On the end was a golden whistle.

The princess explained, "My mother gave that golden whistle to me when I was very small. She said I only had to blow it with the biggest breath my lungs can make, and I would be safe from all harm. Now I want you to have it."

Saul admired the instrument, but then tried to give it back. "Princess, I couldn't possibly."

The princess looked serious. "Young man, don't be rude. Don't you know you should never refuse a gift from a princess?"

Saul's face creased with worry.

Then the princess laughed. She punched him lightly on the shoulder, and said, "I'm just teasing you, silly! But seriously, I want you to have it, so please take it."

"Thank you," Saul replied. "It's an honour." Then he frowned, and asked, "Err... Princess? Why didn't you blow this when you were kidnapped?"

The princess blushed. "It all happened so quickly. This poor old man asked if he could shake my hand, and he looked so innocent that of course I let him – but then a sudden snowstorm swept me away to this land.

"The next thing I knew, I was chained to the table of the six-headed troll. I tried to use the whistle then, but... well. You smelt how awful it was in that hut. Could *you* have drawn the biggest breath your lungs can make in *that* stink?"

"Good point," Saul replied. "Well, thank you so much!" He then tugged on the rope three times, and added, "See you at the top!"

"See you at the top!" she repeated, and blew him a kiss.

As Saul waited for the rope to come back down, he felt something he'd never felt before. It was an odd feeling, made up a bit of missing the princess, and a bit of excitement to see her again soon. He wondered what this feeling could be.

To his surprise, the rope began coming down *fast*.

To his greater surprise, *all* of the rope came down.

The captain had dropped it down the hole! He had clearly decided to take the princess back to the palace without him, and would probably tell everyone he had beaten the troll himself. The cheek! The princess wouldn't go along with that, though, would she? Surely not?

Either way, though, Saul was now stuck in the hole with no way up. He needed to find another way out.

And that's why he had climbed to the top of that tall blue mountain. But even there at the summit, there was still a huge space between him and his own world above. So now he was sitting on the shining blue stone, thinking that he should have listened to his mum.

With a sigh, he dropped his chin into his hands – then felt something cool pressing against his chest…

He sat up straight. Dangling from his neck was…?

The golden whistle!

He drew the deepest breath he could, put the whistle to his lips, and blew.

As the echoes from his toot got quieter and quieter, he heard a sound growing louder out of the distance…

whmph… WHmph… WHMPH…

…and soon, a bird came to rest on a rock beside him, bigger than any bird Saul had ever seen.

Even more amazingly, the bird then spoke.

"*Squell*. You're not the princess."

"No," Saul agreed. "I'm her friend. I rescued her, and she gave me this whistle to say thank you. But now I think *I* need rescuing."

"*Squell*," the bird replied. "I'd like to help you, but there's one slight problem: you're a lot heavier than a princess. You'd need to feed me as we go. Do you have any food?"

Saul sighed. "No. But… what do you eat?"

The bird shrugged. "Oh, any kind of meat really."

Saul had a thought that made him smile.

"How about troll?" he asked.

***

Saul was right: the captain had lifted the princess from the molehill, then dropped the rope to leave Saul behind. At first, the princess protested that she would tell her father – but then the captain said, "If you do, I'll tell him I caught you eating troll porridge!"

The princess fell silent. Troll porridge was known to turn humans mad in three stages: first, the lying stage; next, the dressing-up-in-potato-skins stage; and finally, the killing-everyone-starting-with-the-king-and-queen stage. There was only one cure: having your head chopped off. The princess cared about Saul, but what was the point of caring for someone if you didn't have a head to care with?

So the captain took the princess back to the king and queen of Norway. There in the Great Hall of the palace, the royal parents were overjoyed to see their daughter again – though they couldn't understand why *she* didn't look so happy.

The princess just winced and said, "I feel so silly for shaking that old man's hand!"

The queen smiled fondly. "Don't worry about that, my dear. You're safe now, that's all that matters." Then she turned to the captain. "Good man! As a thank you for rescuing our daughter, we offer you her hand in marriage!"

The princess widened her eyes. "Oh, Mama! Surely the captain won't want to marry me. I've given him enough trouble already."

The king laughed. "Ah, dearest daughter! I'm sure you didn't give the captain the slightest ounce of trouble!"

"None at all!" the captain agreed – and when no-one else was looking, he gave the princess a wicked sneer.

"You see?" the king continued. "And by marrying you, the captain will one day be king, so we can all be happy knowing that a brave and caring warrior will one day rule over our land. What a perfectly happy end– Wait, what's that?"

As the king fell silent, everyone heard a sound increasing in volume from the distance…

whmph… WHmph… WHMPH…

…and then an almighty bird flew in through the highest window. It swooped down to the centre of the

Great Hall, then lowered its head – revealing a boy sat on its back, wearing a golden whistle around his neck.

The queen gasped. "I know that whistle...!"

Saul slid from the bird, then faced the royal family and bowed as low as he could. "Pardon me, your majesties," he said, "but I have come to return the whistle your daughter gave me for rescuing her."

The princess gave a delighted squeal, then ran over to Saul and gave him a *huge* hug. Saul hugged her back, embarrassingly realising *he* had made a delighted squeal too.

Everyone gasped – though the king and queen were grinning with a great glee, elated to see their daughter smiling again.

The princess linked arms with Saul, then turned to the queen and said, "*This* is the man I'd like to marry please, Mama. Remember the dream I told you about a few days ago? This is the boy from that dream! And *he's* the one who *really* rescued me from the troll. If you want a valiant and compassionate warrior to one day rule your kingdom, I can think of no-one finer."

In the presence of Saul and the bird from the golden whistle, the captain knew he wouldn't win an argument. He tried to sneak away, but the palace guards didn't let him get far. He begged the king to let him go, promising to never return. So the king *did* let him go – over the edge of the palace roof, down to the moat below.

And so the princess married Saul. They became the best of friends, often soaring through the sky on thrilling adventures on the back of the bird from the golden whistle. Saul had become an expert at throwing bits of troll into the bird's mouth, keeping it strong enough to carry them both.

In case you're wondering, Saul's mum came to live with them in the palace – so she really *didn't* need to buy another newspaper.

And yes, Saul *did* go back to release the old man from that tree. But what became of the old man after that, no-one knows – even *I* can't tell you.

What I *can* tell you, though, is

that Saul's story was shared across the land of Norway, and grown-ups loved it so much that they told it to their children. Those children loved the story so much that they grew up and told it to *their* children. And eventually a young girl called Sofie Dahl heard the story from *her* grown-up, and she loved Saul's story so much that she never forgot it – even when she left Norway and moved to a country called the United Kingdom.

There in her new home, Sofie Dahl told Saul's story to *her* children: four daughters, called Astri, Alfhild, Else, and Asta; and one son, called Roald.

Roald loved the story so much that he thought about it a *lot*. He wished *he* could go on an adventure like Saul. He *yearned* for adventure so much that, as soon as he left school, he**...?**

...set off to explore Africa. Then he became a fighter pilot. And not long after that, he became**...?**

...a spy!

But listening to his mum tell him Saul's story also helped Roald think creatively, just like Saul and the princess. So you know what Roald did? He used that creativity to**...?**

...invent a medical device! When Roald's own son Theo was hit by a car, Roald's creativity helped him invent a device that the doctors used to save Theo's life – a device that is still being used in hospitals today.

So if listening to Saul's story helped Roald go on to live such a fascinating, varied, and *important* life...

...what could *you* achieve now that *you've* heard it?

Oh, and I nearly forgot to mention. Roald never stopped

thinking about the stories his mum had told him. And inside his head, those stories turned into *even more* stories – stories about *other* children travelling to amazing hidden places, *other* children being remarkably clever, *other* children riding huge talking birds, *other* children getting kidnapped by giants...

So Roald wrote some of those stories down.

Do you know what any of them are called?

Lesson B3:
Where Stories Come From (III)

| **Learning Objective**
What will your learners 'learn', not 'do'? | **Success Criteria**
What must the learners do to be successful? |
|---|---|
| • How some of our favourite authors are inspired by older stories. | • Understand that authors draw on their personal experience when writing.
• Make links between stories. |

Resources

- Paper to record ideas on.
- (Optional) Copies of some books linked to this story, e.g. *Billy and the Minpins*, *The BFG*, *The Lion the Witch and the Wardrobe*, any *Harry Potter* title…

Preparation

- Read the story of '**The Mountain Inside a Molehill**' in advance so you are aware of the content. Consider how you may use VOICE with your learners.

NB: This is the longest story in this collection, and may take more than 30min to read aloud with some groups of learners. For this reason we've made the duration of this lesson highly flexible, and we strongly recommend you make plentiful use of the Conversation key skill to maintain your learners' engagement throughout the reading.

But don't worry – it's a fantastic story that's bound to have your learners hooked till the end!

Starter – *"Do Now!"*
Hooks into learning

Challenge your learners:

> "Draw, write down, or tell your partner about as many Roald Dahl stories as you can think of!"

Main Input

1. Read **'The Mountain Inside a Molehill'** to your learners.

2. Following the final line of the story, ask your learners:

   "Can you think which Roald Dahl stories the writer is referring to?"

   NB: pretty much every Roald Dahl children's book is a valid answer, because they all have heroic and clever children – but the "hidden places", "giant talking birds" and "children getting kidnapped by even bigger giants" might prompt a few specifics.

If a learner makes a suggestion that <u>isn't</u> a Roald Dahl title...
...comment on the difference in author – but express gratitude and excitement for that suggestion, pointing out that other authors might have been influenced by this story too!

If <u>no</u> learner makes a suggestion that isn't a Roald Dahl's title...
...prompt them to do so, e.g. ...

"I wonder if any *other* authors might have taken some ideas from this story?"

"Can we think of any other stories about children travelling to amazing hidden places, for instance...?"

Possible responses are endless. This story definitely influenced C.S.Lewis to conjure *The Chronicles of Narnia*; J.K.Rowling and Phillip Pullman both admit to drawing from folklore to create their respective fantasy novels; there'll doubtlessly be many others.

Independent Activity

Working as individuals, in pairs, or small groups, **challenge** your learners to see who can create the longest list of stories that may have been inspired by all or part of this tale.

Stories from TV, film, and/or video games are valid answers also.

Share ideas from their lists. Has anyone got an idea that no-one else thought of?

Identify which three *books* are the most popular (i.e. on the majority of lists) and available right now, e.g. by putting a tally next to each title that's given, and highlighting the three *books* with the most mentions that you can see/could find in the room right now.

There's more...

Lesson B3: Where Stories Come From (III) All the Better to Read You With

Plenary

Let the winning team select one of three most popular and available books to be the next shared read. Read as much as you can in the remaining time, either from the beginning or from a chapter/scene that your learners feel may have been inspired by part of Saul's story.

If members of that team aren't familiar with some/all of those books, perhaps read the first 2 pages of each book before the winning team votes, as with Lesson A10.

Check In

Talk To Your Partner:

"What have you learnt today?"

Encourage your learners to share their thoughts, but remember: *there's no need to give away the Learning Objective in these lessons.*

Lesson B3:
Behind the Scenes

As you begin to work with the final few lessons in this book, you'll be consolidating a lot of the knowledge *and excitement* your learners have picked up so far. The discussions prompted by this lesson intend to highlight yet further how stories breed stories... stories help us *stay alive, thrive, and be happy*... and even the most famous names rely on old stories for inspiration.

Most learners in the Western world will have encountered the stories of Roald Dahl in one form or another – if not the original books, then on a silver screen, or even onstage. So when you let your learners know that Roald began as an ordinary story listener *just like them*, you encourage them to dream bigger about the impact *they* could have in the world.

That doesn't just have to mean becoming a children's author, though. As the story prompts you to discuss, listening to his mother's stories gave Roald a yearning for adventure that led him to live an incredibly varied life. He definitely thrived – and his son Theo stayed alive – thanks to the creativity imparted in him from his mother's storytelling. Be sure to return to these thoughts when you use the Recyclable 'We Need Stories' lesson on this story.

But whenever we've tried *this* lesson with learners ourselves, it hasn't been long before someone suggests a story written by an author *other* than Roald. And it's easy to see why: CS Lewis, JK Rowling, and Philip Pullman are just some of the major names in children's fiction who have admitted to drawing on folk tales to create their own magical worlds.

By allowing this realisation to stem from your learners, and/or celebrating it when they make that realisation, they will become even more acutely aware of the rich tapestry that is the world of books. The knowledge that a story almost always leads to another will soon manifest as a desire to move from one *book* to another.

And again, when you come to look at creative writing with your learners, if they understand how *published* writers draw on existing work, they'll feel more freedom to do so themselves. With that will come more confidence, too – and that'll be on top of the phrasing fortitude and plotting prowess they'll have harvested in abundance from an increased exposure to written tales.

Of course, it's not just *children's* writers who draw on folklore. Probably the most famous playwright in the history of the world also relied heavily on stories from across the globe. Perhaps that's why his works were originally staged in a theatre *called* 'The Globe'. And in the next lesson, you'll build on everything your learners discovered from Saul's story by sharing yet another huge influence on a huge influence...

The Shapeshifter

Based on English folklore
Adapted & written by Chip Colquhoun,
first published in his book
Cambridgeshire Folk Tales for Children
Illustrated by Mario Coelho

Do you like the names that people call you? Young Robin Goodfellow liked the one his *mum* had given him, but not the one everyone *else* in town called him.

You see, his mum had named him 'Robin', which means 'bright fame' – or, as Robin liked to think of it, 'superstar'! His mum told him he was very special, because he was the son of *the Fairy King*.

Robin had never met his dad, so he had no reason to think his mum was lying – but everyone else thought she was crazy. It's true that Robin's mum was very ill, and she wasn't strong enough to leave the house – so all the other children in the town would laugh at Robin, and tease him by saying, "Your mum's weird, and so are you!"

Even the grown-ups in the town would whisper to each other that there *was* something strange about Robin.

You see, for reasons even Robin didn't understand, animals didn't like him.

When dogs saw Robin, for example, they would suddenly growl and run away. The dogwalkers had to run after them, and often wore themselves out – which of course made those dogwalkers rather cross with Robin.

On other occasions, cats sitting indoors on window ledges would spot Robin walking by outside – and suddenly they'd start climbing the curtains with their claws, ripping the curtains to shreds as they went! The cat owners had to buy new curtains – which made them *really* cross with Robin.

So Robin wasn't very happy. Being teased and scorned made him miserable, and sometimes he got into mischief just to make other people feel as miserable as he did. He began deliberately scaring the farm animals, singing loudly (and badly) outside people's homes when they were trying to enjoy a peaceful evening, and sometimes even chasing and kicking the children who called his mum 'weird' – giving everyone even *more* reasons to dislike him.

That's why everyone else started calling him 'Puck', which means 'gets up to mischief'.

Robin pretended not to care.

But then, at the start of *this* story, the mayor's niece was riding a horse through town when Robin was carrying some food home for his mum. When the horse noticed Robin, it stood up on its two rear legs and neighed loudly, throwing the mayor's niece out from her saddle and into a puddle of muck.

Do you think that was Robin's fault? Everyone there in the town did. Some big strong men quickly grabbed hold of Robin and dragged him to the town square. There, Robin soon found himself surrounded by angry townsfolk – including the mayor.

The mayor's face was as red as the thick red cloak he wore. With a deep, booming voice, he declared, "Puck, you're a menace! What you did today was the worst you've ever done!"

Robin shouted back, "It weren't my fault that stupid horse dropped your crying little niece! I didn' do nothing!"

The mayor sneered. "No-one likes you, Puck. So I'm sending you into exile!"

Robin frowned. "What's 'exile' mean?"

The mayor laughed cruelly. "It means you must leave the town, and never come back!"

Now Robin fell to his knees. "You can't do that! I live here! I need to look after my mum, she doesn't have anyone else! Please!"

But the mayor shrugged. "I can do what I like, lad. And what I'd like to do is make our lives happy... by making you *un*happy!"

With that, the mayor ordered those big strong men to carry Robin to the edge of the town. There they threw him into a ditch, then stomped away laughing.

Robin climbed out of the ditch, on the other side to the town. He was cold, wet, and filthy, and trying hard not to cry. He walked away from the town, but he didn't really know where to go. As it grew dark, he found himself all alone in the middle of a field. So he went and settled by the trunk of a tree to see if he could sleep.

That night, Robin dreamt the strangest dream, in which he saw a man with silver skin, pointy ears, and a crown of leaves. This man said to him, "Robin – I am your father, the Fairy King! I am proud of you, and I think it's time you knew about your fairy powers."

Even in his dream, Robin was surprised. "Fairy powers?" he asked.

"Yes," the Fairy King replied. "You can transform yourself into any creature you want!"

When Robin woke up the next day, he said to himself...

"That were a weird dream."

He didn't think much more about it, though, because he soon had a much more pressing concern: finding something to eat. He'd been sent out from the town before dinner, and without having the chance to pack any food. So now he was in desperate need of nourishment.

Looking up, he saw apples in the tree – but the branches were too high to climb. He thought, *If only I were a bird—*

<u>POOF!</u> Just like that, he *was* a bird!

Robin was surprised and delighted – but still hungry. So he flew straight into the branches of the tree. As a bird, the apples looked a lot bigger – perhaps *too* big for his tiny beak. He thought about being a boy again—

<u>POOF!</u> He turned back into himself again.

As Robin sat in the tree and munched on an apple, he began to think. Could he become *any* creature? He thought of the big men who'd thrown him out of the town—

<u>POOF!</u> And just like that, he looked exactly like one of those men! He was big, and strong...

...and too heavy for the branch!

The wood snapped, and Robin began to fall. He thought of how cats always land on their feet—

<u>POOF!</u> Just like that, he was a cat!

He landed safely on his paws, then turned back into his normal self. He *loved* his new power! He could do whatever he liked now – and having *that* thought made him remember what the mayor had said.

The mayor had said, "I can do what I like, lad. And what I'd like to do is make our lives happy... by making you *un*happy!"

Grinning, Robin said, "Now I can do what *I* like. And what *I'd* like to do is make *my* life happy... by making the mayor and his niece *un*happy!"

With that, Robin transformed himself into a pigeon, and flew back to the town...

Robin flew straight to the mayor's house, where he spotted the niece talking to her boyfriend in the garden. Seeing them gave Robin a really cheeky idea, and he began to fly towards them.

Can you guess what Robin's cheeky idea was? Remember, he had turned himself into a pigeon…

But, as Robin got closer, he heard the niece crying. Between sobs, she said to her boyfriend, "It's just not fair! I want to marry you, but my uncle won't let me! He gives me so many chores, I can never finish them…"

Her boyfriend was crying too. He said to the niece, "I know. When I spoke to him, all he said was, 'I can do what I like, lad. And what I'd like to do is make my life happy… by making you and my niece *un*happy!'"

When Robin heard that, he landed in the garden and turned back into himself. Then he walked over to the niece and her boyfriend and said, "Sounds like someone needs to teach the mayor a lesson!"

The couple jumped. The niece looked as if she was about to scream, so Robin quickly said, "Don't worry! I won't hurt you. I want to teach the mayor that he can't be selfish all the time."

The boyfriend raised an eyebrow. "What can *you* do, Puck? You're just a boy."

Robin smiled, then thought of a bear…

<u>POOF!</u> Just like that, he *was* a bear!

"I think I can convince him," Robin said.

The niece gasped. "But… but… my uncle put you into exile because of me falling off my horse! Are you going to hurt me, too?"

Robin changed back to himself, and shook his head. "It's not your fault your horse got a fright when it saw me. Besides: what I'd like to do is make the *mayor's* life unhappy – and it sounds like I'll do that by making *your* lives *happy!*

"Head to the church, fetch the vicar, and wait for me there. You'll be married today, I promise!"

That made the couple smile! They hurried away, hand-in-hand.

Seeing them looking so happy made *Robin* smile – but then he frowned. He was smiling? He was happy? He was happy because *they* were happy? How curious…

But now they were gone, Robin thought about the mayor's niece—

<u>POOF!</u> And just like that, Robin looked exactly like the mayor's niece! He went into the mayor's house.

The mayor was scoffing his breakfast. When he looked up, he saw Robin – but he *thought* he was seeing his niece. He immediately began bossing Robin about. "Right. Start today with the washing up.

Then get back to your list of chores, you never finish it."

Robin went to bow – but quickly remembered he needed to curtsey. "Of course, uncle," he said. "But first, can I tell you about my amazing dream?"

The mayor frowned. "Your dream?"

Robin nodded. "I dreamt that I *did* finish my chores, all in one day – and you were so happy that you gave me £10! What's more, you then told the vicar I could marry my boyfriend today!"

The mayor laughed. "What a stupid dream! That would never happen – *no-one* could finish all your chores in one day!"

Robin smiled. "But if I *did*... Would you give me £10? And let me marry my boyfriend?"

The mayor laughed even more. "If you achieved the impossible you mean? Ha! I suppose I would!"

"Could we bet on it, then?" Robin asked. "Could you write down on a piece of paper that I can have £10 and marry my boyfriend if I finish all my chores today? And sign it?"

The mayor raised an eyebrow. "But what would be *your* stake?"

Robin bowed his head. "Maybe, if I *don't* finish all my chores today, I could promise to work for you forever?"

The mayor clapped delightedly. "Well, why not! What an easy bet you've given me. Soon you'll be my slave for the rest of my life!"

The mayor wrote out the bet and signed it. Then he left for work, leaving Robin with his huge mansion to clean and tidy...

Washing up the mayor's dirty breakfast plates was easy: **_POOF!_** Robin simply turned into a lion and licked them clean. Well, the mayor would never know, would he...

Then **_POOF!_** Robin metamorphosed into a bird and did some "feather" dusting! **_POOF!_** He moved heavy furniture out of the way as a bear, then **_POOF!_** became a gorilla to beat the carpets. **_POOF!_**

Mole-Robin weeded the flower beds. **_POOF!_** Goat-Robin mowed the lawn (and filled up his stomach over lunch). **_POOF!_** Octopus-Robin quickly spun and squeezed the mayor's clothes clean in the bathtub, and **_POOF!_** Robin discovered he could even become a dragon, so he could blow some fire to get the clothes dry.

Robin finished all the jobs with a whole hour to spare – so he turned back into the mayor's niece, then lay on the sofa and read the newspaper until the mayor came home.

When the mayor later returned through the front door, his mouth dropped open.

Robin smiled. "So... Can I have my £10 please?"

The mayor snarled, and rushed to the table where he'd left the piece of paper with the bet written on it.

Robin guessed that the mayor was about to tear the bet in half. So Robin thought of a frog...

POOF! And just like that, he turned into a frog! His long tongue whipped out and he snatched the bet away from the mayor's outstretched hand.

The mayor yelped, and turned to see where the tongue had come from. When he saw the frog transform back into his niece, the mayor screamed, and he began running back to the front door...

...but **_POOF!_** Lion-Robin pounced in front of him! He growled, and said, "Give me my £10..."

Whimpering, the terrified mayor pulled a £10 note from his wallet.

Lion-Robin grinned at the sight of the money and the cowering mayor – but then wondered if he could turn into a bird big enough to carry the mayor...

POOF! And just like that, he did!

The mayor couldn't stop screaming as Robin carried him all the way to the church, where the mayor's niece and her boyfriend were waiting with the vicar.

Everyone gasped as Robin dropped the mayor to the ground. Then he metamorphosed back to his normal self and handed the piece of paper with the bet to the vicar, saying "Here: this proves that the mayor is happy for his niece to marry this young man now all the mayor's chores are done."

The mayor was lying on the ground, shivering, and still clutching the £10 note. Robin calmly walked over, took the money, then passed it to the niece, saying, "Here: this is so you can start your life together as a rich couple!"

£10 was a lot of money in those days – enough for the niece and her boyfriend to buy their first house together. The couple were delighted, and hugged – but then both turned to Robin.

"Thank you, Puck!" they said. "Thank you so much!"

Robin was about to say, "My name's not Puck!" – but he didn't. Instead, he realised: apart from his mum, no-one had ever thanked him before.

That realisation filled Robin with pride, and he almost smiled wide enough to push his ears off his head. And besides – he *had* been mischievous. He had tricked the mayor using his superpower, and being tricky was a type of mischief. So maybe 'Puck' was a good name for him after all.

It could be his special name... His *superstar* name!

And so, 'Puck' decided it was time to leave. He changed into a robin (the bird this time), feeling like the most happiest boy in the world... *ever!*

Then as he flew away, Puck thought to himself...

From now on, I'm going to make my life happy... by making **other people** *happy!*

And you know, Puck is still doing that today. Have you ever lost something, but then suddenly found it again? That was probably Puck finding it for you, then placing it where you would come across it. Has something ever fallen over suddenly, and made you laugh? That was probably Puck trying to give you a giggle. Have you ever heard the sound of a person or an animal, gone to look, but found no-one there? That might have been Puck tricking you into moving so he could save you from a disaster...

Sometimes he even works with his father, the King of the Fairies, who gives him special missions – like the midsummer night when he was asked to help a group of women and men fall in love with the right people. *That* story got turned into a play by a fellow called Shakespeare, and many more people have been made happy by watching it.

Perhaps you've heard of it?

Lesson B4:
Where Stories Come From (IV)

Learning Objective *What will your learners 'learn', not 'do'?*	**Success Criteria** *What must the learners do to be successful?*
• How pretty much *all* authors are inspired by older stories!	• Understand that authors draw on their personal experience when writing. • Make links between stories.

Resources

- Copies of the list of words Shakespeare invented.
- Paper to record ideas on.
- Copies of some books linked to this story, e.g. any *Harry Potter* title, any *X-Men* comic featuring Mystique, stories with werewolves and vampires…
- (For the Optional Extra) Copies of the lines from the story set against the lines from *A Midsummer Night's Dream*.

Preparation

- Read the story of '**The Shapeshifter**' in advance so you are aware of the content. Consider how you may use VOICE with your learners.
- Depending on the knowledge level of your learners, you may wish to let them watch or read an adaptation of *A Midsummer Night's Dream* prior to this lesson.

Starter – "Do Now!"
Hooks into learning

Share the list of words created by Shakespeare with your learners and invite them to talk/think/draw/write a sentence using at least one of these words.

Prior Knowledge Check

Instruct your learners:

"Talk/think/draw/write about any stories which link to things that have happened to you."

Main Input

1. Read **'The Shapeshifter'** to your learners.

2. (Optional) If any of your learners are aware of *A Midsummer Night's Dream*, ask:

   "What are some of the things that Puck gets up to in *A Midsummer Night's Dream*?"

   Ensure the following points are drawn out, recalling details yourself if they are not suggested by your learners:

   - Pretending to be other people.
   - Giving someone the head of a donkey.
   - Conjuring a fog to cause people to bump into the 'right' partners.

   Then ask:

   "Do you think Puck was helping or having fun with them?"
   "Why do you think that?"

3. Ask your learners,

   "What other stories were possibly influenced by Puck? Do you know any other stories with shapeshifting, helpful fairies, and/or trickery?"

   As with Lesson B3, the possible responses are endless. Shapeshifters abound in popular franchises including *X-Men*, *Twilight*, *Harry Potter*, etc, and tricksters are even more common.

   NB: *If anyone mentions a mythological trickster, such as Loki from the Norse, you could comment on how those myths were around <u>before</u> Puck – so maybe the legends of Puck were influenced by <u>them</u>...*

There's more...

Independent Activity

Working as individuals, in pairs, or small groups, **challenge** your learners to see who can create the longest list of stories that may have been inspired by all or part of this tale.

Stories from TV, film, and/or video games are valid answers also.

Share ideas from their lists. Has anyone got an idea that no-one else thought of?

Identify which three *books* are the most popular (i.e. on the majority of lists) and available right now, e.g. by putting a tally next to each title that's given, and highlighting the three *books* with the most mentions that you can see/could find in the room right now.

Plenary

Let the winning team select one of three most popular and available books to be the next shared read. Read as much as you can in the remaining time, either from the beginning or from a chapter/scene that your learners feel may have been inspired by part of Puck's story.

If members of that team aren't familiar with some/all of those books, perhaps read the first 2 pages of each book before the winning team votes, as with Lesson A10.

Optional Extra

Give your learners the sheet of lines from the story and lines from *A Midsummer Night's Dream*, then instruct them to compare the characters of Puck between them.

For example: in '**The Shapeshifter**', Puck changes into animals; in *A Midsummer Night's Dream*, he changes into stools.

Check In

Talk To Your Partner:

> "What have you learnt today?"

Encourage your learners to share their thoughts, but remember: *there's no need to give away the Learning Objective in these lessons.*

Words that Shakespeare *made up!*

- aerial
- armgaunt
- barefaced
- bodikins
- catlike
- dauntless
- dwindle
- eftes
- enrapt
- fitful
- gallantry
- gust
- hedge-pig
- hobnail
- impeticos
- insisture
- keech
- kickie-wickie
- leapfrog
- monumental
- mortifying
- newsmonger
- oppugnancy
- pajock
- pioned
- rawboned
- ribaudred
- tanling
- wappened
- zany

...and there were many more!

Puck in 'The Shapeshifter'...

"When dogs saw Robin, they would suddenly growl and run away – which of course made the dogwalkers rather cross."

"Robin dreamt the strangest dream, in which a man with silver skin and a crown of leaves said, "Robin – I am your father, the Fairy King! I think it's time you knew about your fairy powers."

"With that, Robin transformed himself into a pigeon, and flew back to the town…"

"…just like that, Robin looked exactly like the mayor's niece! He went into the mayor's house."

Puck in *A Midsummer Night's Dream*...

FAIRY: Robin Goodfellow! Isn't it you who plays pranks on the girls who work in the village, making them breathless by stopping the milk from turning into butter no matter how much they churn? Don't you lead people out at night the wrong way, and laugh at them?

PUCK: That's right, that's me! I tell jokes to the Fairy King and make him smile. Sometimes I'll trick a horse into thinking *I'm* a horse. Sometimes I hide at the bottom of an old gossipy woman's cup in the form of an apple. When she drinks, I bob against her lips so that she spills the beer. Sometimes an old woman telling a sad story will think I'm a stool – then when she tries to sit on me, I slip out and she falls down, and everyone around holds their bellies and laughs, and none of them has ever had more fun…"

Seething at the Sea

Based on Aesop's Fable
Adapted & written by Chip Colquhoun
Illustrated by Mario Coelho

Even before he opened his eyes, Michael knew something wasn't right. His body was lying still and flat on something solid, but his head felt like it was rolling round and around and around.

The rolling wasn't actually unusual – he was a sailor after all, and sleeping on a ship often felt like rolling around. But the odd thing was, right now, Michael *wasn't on* a ship.

On a ship, he'd be sleeping in a hammock. Being a sheet pinned at two ends above the floor, a hammock never felt solid. Whatever he was lying on now? That was solid.

He half-opened his eyelids – then immediately shut them again. The Sun was directly above him, and there was no roof or cloud to block its blindingly bright light from hitting his eyes. He rolled onto one side before daring to open his eyelids again, and straight away he was sick.

He groaned. His tummy ached, and so did his head – but even so, he took a moment to thank the Sun for forcing him to roll over. Otherwise, all that sick would have spurted from his mouth like a fountain, then splattered back down onto his face.

Now, he took in his surroundings. Sand, so much sand. A clump of thin palm trees. A slight breeze cooling his sunburnt skin. The sound of waves gently lapping at the shore – and his feet...

Yipe! He scrabbled away from the water's edge. That tickled!

He sat up, rubbed his eyes, and gaped.

He was sitting on the beach of an island surrounded by sea – miles and miles and maybe millions of miles of sea.

Michael scrambled to his feet and looked around. The island was so small, he could look between the palm trees and see the sea on the other side too. A few broken bits of his ship had washed up with him, and luckily a chest as well – though what was in that chest, Michael couldn't yet be sure. If clothes, maybe he could bandage up the various cuts he had all over his body. If food, he could enjoy more nutrition than just the coconuts from the palm trees. If treasure…

What use was treasure? Reflecting sunlight onto some sticks to start a fire maybe? Then perhaps he could attract a passing ship over to rescue him?

He looked back out across the endless sea.

Attract *what* passing ship? Apart from the palm trees and fish, there wasn't any life for miles around! Not even a bird!

Michael suddenly felt helpless – a feeling which quickly changed to anxiety. He could die here! He didn't *want* to die! He kicked up a cloud of sand and cried, *"I don't want to die!"*

He stamped forward until his bare feet splashed back into the waves lapping across the damp sand. *"D'you hear me?"* he screeched. *"I DON'T WANT TO DIE!"*

Tears burst from his eyes, but he quickly slapped them away with his hand and wiped his sleeve across his nose. He was a sailor. Sailors didn't cry. Sailors got *angry*.

"Stupid sea!" he shouted. "Why? Why did you do this to us, to me? Why? Why'd you lift up your waves to the height of houses, then batter our boards from side to side? What had we ever done to you? Hey?"

Now Michael was stamping as he spoke, and pounding his hips with his fists.

"It's all your fault!" he continued to cry. "You tricked us! You lay there, all calm and blue and peaceful, a serene sea – 'So alright!' we said. 'Let's set sail today!' we said. But as soon as we'd sailed so far we couldn't see our home no more, that's when you did it! Raised your watery arms and… *CRASH!* Smashing against our sides till we couldn't stand, sloshing your waters across our decks till we couldn't get up, then digging your salty

fingernails in and *pulling our ship apart! Why? WHY?! Answer me, WHY?!"*

It was a gentle, womanly voice that spoke back to him: "Now just hold your tongue, young man."

Michael froze. The Sun was hot, but he suddenly felt an icy chill down his back. Even so, he dared not shiver. Just moments before, he had looked all around himself – all three hundred and sixty degrees. No woman could be thin enough to hide behind the trunk of a palm tree. There weren't any caves. He could see the chest from the corner of his eye, and the lid was shut tight.

So who said that? he thought – though he was too nervous to say it out loud.

"Over here," said the voice.

Michael slowly turned his head towards the sound – and there, rising up from the sea, was a woman.

No, *not* rising up from the sea – that would make her something like a mermaid, or some other kind of woman who could live underwater and occasionally poke her head above the surface. This woman *was* the sea: the water swirled into the shape of her dress, and somehow took on a shimmering bluey-green sheen from which her light blue arms and head extended.

Her face had a beauty so gorgeous it made Michael feel shy, but her expression looked upset – making Michael feel guilty for some reason. This expression was framed by thick green curls of hair – no, *seaweed*, but it *looked* like hair. Resting at the top of her forehead was a tiara made of the shiniest shells surrounding the prettiest, most perfect pearl.

"What–" Michael began – then stopped himself, and started again. "*Who...* Who are you?"

The woman looked even *more* upset. "Why, I'm the Sea!"

Michael blinked. "You're the Sea."

The woman nodded. "Yes."

Michael blinked twice more. "I'm talking to... the Sea?!"

Now the woman rolled her eyes. "You didn't seem to have a problem *shouting* at me a moment ago! But now I stand before you, and suddenly you're surprised to see me?"

Blinking clearly wasn't working, so Michael rubbed his eyes – but when he looked out again, the woman was still there. Was she a dream caused by his exhaustion? A mirage caused by the heat? A hallucination caused by a knock to his head?

"No," she replied, even though he hadn't said anything. "I'm the Sea. And you, young man, asked me to answer you."

Michael shook his head in wonder. "I... I did."

"You accused me," the Sea went on, "of luring you onto my calm, peaceful, serene surface, and waiting for you to travel too far from home before using my largest waves to bash your vessel around."

Michael nodded slowly – then, remembering his rage, he nodded more firmly. "That's right, I did. And then you pulled our ship apar–"

"No!" the Sea suddenly cried, clenching her hands like a baby having a strop. "I did *not!* Stop accusing me of things that aren't my fault!"

Michael felt that guilt again. "I... But..."

"You can't blame me!" the Sea went on. "I *am* calm, I *am* peaceful, and I *am* serene – just like the rest of the Earth! It's the *Wind* you should be seething against. The Wind lashes my surface, hoisting up those waves as huge as houses, then thrusting them against the sides of your vessel. It's the *Wind* you should blame for beating your boat apart, and leaving you stranded here on this deserted desert island."

The End

"What?" Michael said. "Hey, wait a minute!"

"Yes!" the Sea added. "This story can't end there!"

Um... The Writer wasn't sure what to do at this point.

"You're not sure what to do?!" Michael replied incredulously. "Keep telling the story, of course!"

"That's right!" the Sea added. "Nothing's even happened yet!"

Now look, wrote the Writer. That's not fair. Something *has* happened, thank you very much. We know that good stories need something bad to happen, and something bad *has* happened: a sailor has been stranded. And we also know that good stories have a message for us. Well, this story has the message that you should be careful who you blame. Michael blamed the Sea for his shipwreck, but it wasn't her fault – it was the Wind.

Michael raised his arms. "So? What now?"

The Writer was confused. What do you mean, 'What now?'?

"I *mean* exactly what you wrote I said!" Michael replied. "I mean, I'm here on this island. Something bad hasn't *happened* – it's *still happening!*"

"Exactly!" the Sea added. "And what's the point in this young man learning a lesson about who to blame if he's just going to sit in the sand and do nothing with his new knowledge?"

The Writer shrugged. Well don't blame me, the Writer wrote. This story is thousands of years old – I'm just rewriting it for people who are alive today. When this story was *first* written, I guess the original writer thought you two just didn't matter as much as the folks reading and listening to the story. *They* are the ones who are supposed to enjoy the bad thing and the message – not you.

"Hmm," the Sea said. "And do the good people reading and listening to this story think that's fair?"

"Aye," Michael agreed. "What do *they* think should happen now?"

The Writer began to wonder the same thing.

So...

What do *you* think should happen next?

Lesson B5:
Stories Need *Us*...

Learning Objective	Success Criteria
What will your learners 'learn', not 'do'?	*What must the learners do to be successful?*
• Just how much *we* are influenced by stories.	• Understand that authors draw on their personal experience when writing. • Make links between stories. • Understand that their *own* writing is influenced by their own experiences.

Resources

- Reading/Writing journals.

Preparation

- Read the story of **'Seething at the Sea'** in advance so you are aware of the content. Consider how you may use VOICE with your learners. **NB: You need to keep reading aloud to your learners all the words *after* "The End"!**

Starter – *"Do Now!"*
Hooks into learning

Instruct your learners:

"Think of stories you have read, seen on TV, or had read to you that involve shipwrecks, and draw/write/talk about them."

Main Input

Read **'Seething at the Sea'** to your learners.

Following the *actual* final line of the story, encourage your learners to predict what they think should happen next, keeping the following questions in mind...

1. Should the Message be to help people (a) stay alive, (b) thrive, or (c) be happy?

2. How will the story give that Message?

3. Does the story need anything else Bad to happen?

(Optional) As part of this discussion, you may wish to explore what other stories your learners know that involve shipwrecks, and consider what Messages are in those. Popular examples might be *Treasure Island, Kensuke's Kingdom, Robinson Crusoe*, etc.

Independent Activity

Working as individuals, in pairs, or small groups, **challenge** your learners to plan a better ending for the tale.

Scaffold: they can also draw and/or act out their ideas.

Plenary

1. Encourage your learners to share their ideas.

2. Discuss whether your learners' ideas really are better than Aesop's original ending.

3. Ask your learners to explain where they got their ideas from.

The aim is to show that hearing stories has made them better story makers – and so, like a certain caveman called Huh, they should now be able to go on helping human beings to survive – for another...? **<u>Forty thousand years!</u>**

Check In

Talk To Your Partner:

"What have you learnt today?"

Encourage your learners to share their thoughts, but remember: *there's no need to give away the Learning Objective in these lessons.*

Lesson B5:
Behind the Scenes

Our final lesson in this book is both an ending and a beginning. On the one hand, you're consolidating everything your learners have discovered along the Upper Pathway: the importance of the Bad Thing, the relevance of stories to our survival as human beings, and the influence of stories on subsequent storytellers.

But of course, in this final lesson, those subsequent storytellers are your learners themselves. Just like folklore bred the creativity of Julia Donaldson, Roald Dahl, Shakespeare *et al*, this lesson provides the opportunity to reveal just how creative your learners have become after this journey of discovery through reading. That's why, at the end, you will easily tie it in with Huh's 'Most Incredible Thought' – and imply that they, your learners, are creating humanity's chances of survival for the future.

So from here, you're perfectly positioned to launch your learners into a course on creative writing – one they're likely to be highly enthusiastic to embark upon, spurred on by their newfound love of reading and the language that writers use. Now they're regularly recognising a writer's rhetoric and identifying key components of plots, they'll be soaking up those techniques and ideas – *not* like a sponge, but like a *paintbrush*, ready to practice deploying those same techniques and ideas in their *own* writing.

This shouldn't be the end of your reading adventures, though – and your learners probably won't let it be! That's why, if you haven't done so already, we recommend you now flick back to Volume A and take your learners through Lesson A10: *What's Going to Happen? (II)*. Let *them* determine your next class read, and you'll have them excitedly and attentively engrossed in further fantastical adventures...

...to the *huge* benefit of their future selves.

Final Words? What Next

Once you've taken your learners through one of the Pathways in this book, perhaps using the VOICE key skills but *always* using your *keyring* skill, you can be confident that they have begun to associate the act of reading with pleasure.

So what now?

You should *now* be able to introduce a *successful* daily 15min of independent reading per day. Unlike the learners in the Australian study mentioned in our introduction, your learners will begin with an *experiential appreciation* for the opportunity you're providing them.

Or how about going one further, and introducing a daily 15min of *reading to each other*? Remember: learners love finding out what their friends and peers are passionate about, because it sets up an *expectation of pleasure*. So if they're listening to each other share the stories they enjoy, their enjoyment for the activity will be amplified.

Why not do both? If time is short, provide 10min of independent reading followed by 5min of one learner sharing a passage they've especially enjoyed with everyone else.

And now, given what you've discovered in this book about the educational benefits of reading for pleasure *and* the incredibly engaging, effective teaching tool that is storytelling... can you imagine how much your learners' cross-curricular knowledge and understanding will improve if you start applying story, storytelling, and the pleasure principle in all other areas of learning too?

Look out for the next handbooks in the *All the Better to* series – and the Educator Editions on Chip and Korky's *Fables & Fairy Tales* series – and you'll soon achieve just that. But in the meantime, why wait? Dig out books for young readers on the subjects you need to cover, ideally fiction, and start those lessons with some shared reading. Use the Recyclable lessons in this book on those stories too. Continue to enthuse about those stories as much as you've enthused about the ones we've given you here. Sit back and smile as the natural engagement and enthusiasm inspired by story compels your learners into rapidly increasing their interest and aptitude in all areas of their education.

The success of sharing stories with your learners is the story of your learners' success.

Share Your Story-Led Journey

However you've got on with the stories and lessons in this handbook, please let us know! We'd love to hear your thoughts, questions, and results.

To do this, send a message to **Epic Tales** on Facebook, Instagram, LinkedIn and X using the handle **@EpicTalesST**, or find the latest contact information at **epictales.co.uk**.

You can also connect with Chip for further tips on storytelling, writing, and reading for pleasure – including how to be nominated for the Society of Authors' Reading for Pleasure Award – by visiting **storytellerchip.com**.

Right now, then, it only remains for us to say cheerio, and we hope to hear *your* story soon. So...

Cheerio!

And we hope to hear *your* story soon...!

Appendix:

Recyclable Lessons

Recyclable Lesson 1:
Fun on the Page

Learning Objective
What will your learners 'learn', not 'do'?

- To explore, and delight in, the sound of words, then link that delight to reading.

Success Criteria
What must the learners do to be successful?

- Explore new words.
- Choose words that they take delight in.
- Explore the sounds words make.

Resources

- Paper and drawing/colouring materials.
- Magpie sheet for children's sketches/ideas/magpied words (see the original Lesson A3 for a version of this sheet to photocopy).

Preparation

- Read your chosen shared read in advance so you are aware of the content. Consider how you may use VOICE with your learners.

Starter – *"Do Now!"*
Hooks into learning

Give groups of learners a list of 9 words that they can read (these need to be matched with the level your learners are working at) and ask them to rank these words with their favourite word first. They need to be able to explain why they have put them in that order, and why the top word is their favourite.

Prior Knowledge Check

Talk To Your Partner:

"Have you discovered any new favourite words recently? What do they mean?"

Encourage your learners to share their thoughts.

Main Input

1. Read your chosen text to all your learners together.

2. Talk To Your Partner:

   "What did you like about the text and why?"

   Record the children's ideas for your reading wall.

3. Talk To Your Partner:

   "What *language/words/vocabulary* in the text do you like?"

   Lead with a few of your favourite examples (moments of rhyme, alliteration, 'fun-sounding' words, moments of surprise).

NB: You and your learners may find it useful to re-read the text in manageable chunks. Alternatively, as you go through the text the first time, you can stop and discuss after each section.

Independent Activity

Instruct your learners to record their favourite words and/or phrases on a magpie sheet. They may include illustrations as well.

Scaffold: Print out the text so that learners can highlight and copy the parts they want to magpie.

Challenge/Stretch: Ask your learners to define the words they have selected, either by using a dictionary or inferring from the context of the words in the sentence.

Plenary

Share the words/phrases the children have selected to magpie and add some of them to your reading wall.

Check In

Talk To Your Partner:

"What have you learnt today?"

Encourage your learners to share their thoughts, but remember: *there's no need to give away the Learning Objective in these lessons.*

Recyclable Lesson 2: What a Story Needs

Learning Objective	**Success Criteria**
What will your learners 'learn', not 'do'?	*What must the learners do to be successful?*
• How to identify the first essential element of a good story: the *Bad Thing*.	• Identify "bad things" that happen in stories. • Understand how these are actually important for a story. • Unpick a story of their choice (i.e. identify how the "bad things" are important for that story).

Resources

- (Optional) A table (either on a board or flipchart) with 2 columns – one headed "I don't like it when…", the other headed "…but that's good because…"
- A worksheet version of this table for your learners.

Preparation

- (Optional) Take some time to look through the story you're sharing with your learners to identify at least one Crisis Point yourself that you can use as an example.
- If you are using this lesson with a longer text, consider the best passage to use.
  NB: With chapter books, it can sometimes be a while before the main Crisis Point arrives; however, from the perspective of encouraging reading for pleasure, it can be more effective to use this lesson early on (maybe even with the first chapter) to help your learners identify what elements in the main character's day-to-day life could be improved.

Starter – "Do Now!"
Hooks into learning

Instruct your learners to write/draw/discuss the answer to this question:

"What were the bad things that happened in the last story we shared? Be ready to share what you have remembered."

Prior Knowledge Check

Share the bad things that your learners have remembered from the story, and draw their attention to any that they have not remembered.

Main Input

1. Explain that you're going to read the story again (or, with a longer text, a passage), but this time your learners should stop you if they spot a Crisis Point in the story, i.e. something bad happening that could be taken out. NB: The first one or two times you use this Recyclable lesson, you may find it useful to have at least one example from early in the story to explain the concept, such as...

   ...in the story of '**Tiger's Terror**', the first Bad Thing might be the tiger jumping out at the fox.

   ...in the story of '**The Mountain Inside a Molehill**', the first Bad Thing might be the knight captain tricking Saul into being 'bait'.

   ...in the story of **Harry Potter and the Philosopher's Stone**, the first Bad Thing might be the Dursleys bullying Harry.

2. Agree a sign that your learners can use to let you know when they think the story is at a crisis point, then begin to re-read the story/passage.

3. When a learner pauses the story, ask them to explain why they think this is a Crisis Point.

4. If anyone else in the group agrees, add this to a list of Crisis Points, then continue with the tale.

After reaching the end of your text/passage, ask your learners to Talk To Your Partner:

"Do you think the characters would have had a happy ending without these challenges? Why/why not?"

5. Remind your learners of the "I don't like it when / but that's good because" table. NB: The first one or two times you use this Recyclable lesson, you may find it useful to work through the first Crisis Point as an example – such as...

   ...if the tiger hadn't jumped out, the fox couldn't have shown how clever he was.

   ...if the captain hadn't tricked Saul, they might have gone into the hole as friends, and the princess might have fallen in love with the strong and heroic captain.

   ...if the Dursleys hadn't been bullies, Harry might have felt happy at home and decided not to go to Hogwarts.

There's more...

Independent Activity

Instruct your learners to complete the table, either as pairs, groups, or on their own.

Plenary

Share your learners' independent activity, perhaps under a visualizer. Do any learners have anything to add to each other's tables?

Check In

Talk To Your Partner:

"What have you learnt today?"

Encourage your learners to share their thoughts, but remember: *there's no need to give away the Learning Objective in these lessons.*

...but that's good because...

I don't like it when...

Recyclable Lesson 3: We Need Stories

Learning Objective
What will your learners 'learn', not 'do'?

- How to identify the *second* essential element of a good story: the *Message*.

Success Criteria
What must the learners do to be successful?

- Understand the Message in a given story.
- Share their ideas.

Resources

- Reading/Writing journals.

Starter – *"Do Now!"*
Hooks into learning

Instruct your learners:

"Discuss, draw, or write about what you can remember from the last story we shared."

Prior Knowledge Check

Ask your learners:

"What lessons did *you* learn from this story?"

Main Input

1. After bringing back to mind the importance of stories for helping us "stay alive, thrive, or be happy," lead a discussion with your learners about the Messages in your latest shared read.

2. Invite your learners to consider the following points for discussion:

    "Is there any way the writer could have made the Message more obvious?"

    "Do you like the Message? Could the story have had a better one?"

    "How would the story be different if the Message changed?"

    "How would the Message change if the *Bad Thing* changed?"

    *NB: For that last question, you could use some of your learners' ideas for alternative Crisis Point resolutions from **Recycled Lesson 2: What a Story Needs**.*

Independent Activity

Either...

- Invite your learners to record the Message(s) in your latest shared read using their Reading/Writing Journal.

...and/or...

- Invite your learners to write/draw/act their alternative stories to produce different/enhanced Messages.

Plenary

- Invite your learners to share their work/presentations with each other, and/or the group as a whole.

Check In

Talk To Your Partner:

"What have you learnt today?"

Encourage your learners to share their thoughts, but remember: *there's no need to give away the Learning Objective in these lessons.*

Acknowledgements

So many people had a part in bringing this book into being that it would be impossible to name them all without doubling its page count. But the two greatest and longest-serving influences are the first and best storytellers I ever met – *aka* Mummy and Gaggy. Their support throughout my storytelling endeavours has been both a safety net and a trampoline.

The next biggest influence began when Amy Scott Robinson asked me to help her set up a small storytelling business way back in 2007. Neither of us knew quite where that would lead… Amy's impact on this book goes far beyond the witty and wonderful 'Through the Forest', and I'm deeply in her debt.

Then there are all my incredible storytelling mentors. The traditional storytelling community is an incredibly vibrant, varied, and generous one – it's all about passing on stories, after all – and I've learned so much from so many. There's not enough space to list them all here, especially since worldstorytellingcafe.com brought so many more of us together during the covid pandemic – but key individuals who inspired and encouraged me from the start include Tony Cooper, John Hardwick, Bob Hartman, Graham Langley, Mary Medlicott, John Row, and Christine Willison. And others who particularly supported *this* book were Pauline Cordiner (with Molly and Nat), Donald Nelson, and Janina Vigurs. Thank you all.

I've been both influenced and inspired by the hundreds of thousands of eager young listeners I've met throughout the years, in schools, theatres, festivals, museums, hospitals, department stores… even the back of a bus! This includes Jan and Luke, whose stories can be found in Ch2, and Bethany, who contributed the awesome portrait for Ch5. Mahoosive thanks to these folks especially, and their families for allowing me to include their stories in this book.

Storytelling in schools gave me the privilege to meet innumerable teachers who inspire awe through their knowledge, patience, and superhuman dedication to their learners. Again, there are too many to mention them all here – but those without whom this book would most certainly have stalled include Jo Phillips, Rae Snape, and the incredibly inventive hivemind that was the core *Happily Ever Teaching* team: Toria Bono, Caitlin Bracken, Nicola Collings, Laura-Jayne Hare, Abi Marrison, Helen Simpson, Rob Small, and of course the brilliant Bex.

Bex gets a whole paragraph to herself, of course, as without her this book just wouldn't have been able to exist. Cheers, Texter Bexter! $;-D

Although I'd dreamt of this book for years, it still needed a few people to entice it out of my head and into reality. The first of these were ShaliniDevi Ramanathan and Jigna Dharod from India, whose enthusiasm was as invaluable as their early advice on what should be included. They helped me build the fire; it was then lit by Mel Rose, Marie Powell, and Jacky Briscoe of the National English Hub. Here I must also thank Dan Lentell and daughter Elsie, whose keen interest in my storytelling since coming to see my performance at the Edinburgh Fringe in 2018 is what brought me to Mel and Marie's attention – and also led me to live in the old home of Samuel Pepys!

Huge thanks to Korky and Mario, who never fail to bowl me over with their brilliance, as well as their enthusiasm and support throughout (plus an incredibly tasty Greek lunch). This book really was enhanced beyond measure with the colour, creativity and wit that slides off their paintbrushes.

Significant support came from my Springboard pals at the National Centre for Writing: Megan Bradbury, Leigh Chambers, Lynn Fraser, Maddy Glen, Jenny Knight, Joy Martin, Ella Micheler, Ben Scott, Elena Traina, David Vass, Rob Wright, and the genius who brought us all together, Sam Ruddock. And support of similarly tough stock came from my fellow 'Scooby' and writing accountability partner Matt Kileen, whose daily injections of wit and enccuragement helped manifest this book into being. Writing can be a solitary profession, but it shouldn't be, and these folks kept me going through the toughest climes.

Speaking of tough climes... Terrible writer that I am, I deeply appreciated the eagle eyes of Aleki Russell – huge thanks to him for correcting our copious errors, and helping Bex and me sound almost like professionals. Gratitude also to those who highlighted further great gaffs in advance reads: Jane Bower, Ros Wilson, Claire Winterbottom, and the super smart William Crankshaw who pointed out that a bison wouldn't be found in India (it's now been replaced, correctly, by a gaur).

And yes, I'm pretty sure Ros did a spot of proof-reading just to make sure she got acknowledged twice. $;-) I was hugely honoured and excited when she agreed to write our foreword, and am exceedingly grateful to her for the words and support she's put into these pages.

This book almost definitely wouldn't have happened at all without the energy and generosity from the Immersive Experiences/Epic Tales team, specifically the dapper David Ault and the amazing Zee Dinally.

Uniting all this influence, though, is the unending strength I receive from my wife Emma and our kittens Tito and Pippa. They've fuelled this book with mugs of tea, plentiful purrs, tasty treats, regular huge hugs, and a skipload of patience – all of which have been essential.

Yup – you wouldn't be enjoying this book had it not been for the influence, impact, and/or encouragement of everyone named above. So I wholeheartedly thank them all – and also *you*, since a book is worthless without someone to read it. So thank *you* mahoosively, and may this work and everything that's gone into it be of bountiful benefit to you and those you care for.

– Chip

I'd like to begin by thanking my Robins past present and future, to whom I've also dedicated this book, for allowing me to share wonderful stories with them, and for making me a better teacher each day. Everything I've brought to this book has been because of them.

Thanks also to Dad and Mum, who have always believed in me.

And finally, huge thanks to Esther, Fran, Craig, Nickie, Hannah and my floofs, Sybil, Cedric, and Star. In their own amazing and unique ways, each was instrumental in supporting me along the incredible and fun journey that's brought me to this point – so thank you so much!

– Rebekah

About Your Storytellers

Chip Colquhoun began storytelling professionally in 2007 alongside Amy Scott Robinson. He's since performed in 10 countries, presented Traditional Tales for the Oxford Reading Tree online, performed regularly at Glastonbury Festival, and represented the Roald Dahl Story Museum on ITV. He also wrote the EU's guidance on using storytelling in schools. He lives in the former residence of Samuel Pepys, England's most famous diarist, up in Cambridgeshire with his wife Emma and kitten Tito.

During her 20 years at Cambridgeshire's Little Paxton Primary School, **Rebekah Owen** has held various roles, and is currently Deputy Head. She has taught classes throughout the primary age range, but her first passion is always ensuring that her learners receive a rich and varied reading diet. Her second passion is in supporting both trainee teachers and various members of staff through the various stages of their careers, and she has been a trainer with the Cambridge Training School Network's School Centred Initial Teacher Training programme since its inception. So she was excited and delighted to blend these passions by becoming a regular contributor to the *Happily Ever Teaching* podcast soon after she met Chip during the 2020 pandemic.

Korky Paul began his career scribbling for an advertising agency in Cape Town. His first illustration job was a book teaching English, then a pop-up called *The Crocodile and the Dumper Truck* – but it was his work on *Winnie the Witch* that won the Children's Book Award in 1987 and made him a much-loved figure in the world of children's books. He's since illustrated for Oxford University Press, Penguin, Random House, and others. He lives in Oxford with his wife Susan.

Mario Coelho was born on the Brazilian island of Florianopolis. He worked as an artist and designer in the textile industry before moving to England in 1985. After completing a course in children's book illustration run by Korky Paul, Mario began receiving several commissions, starting with an edition of Oscar Wilde's *The Canterville Ghost* published by Oxford University Press. For more examples of his work, or to commission him yourself, visit mariocoelho.co.uk

Milton Keynes UK
Ingram Content Group UK Ltd.
UKHW021433120124
435920UK00002B/3